Pursuit of Happiness

A Left Bank Book

Edited by
Linny Stovall

Blue Heron Publishing, Inc. • Hillsboro, Oregon

Pursuit of Happiness
A Left Bank Book

Copyright © 1995 by Blue Heron Publishing, Inc.
Left Bank Books is an imprint of Blue Heron
Publishing, Inc. All rights reserved.

ISBN 0-936085-30-4

Editor: Linny Stovall

Editorial Assistants: Mary C. Miller, Peter Sears, William Woodall

Proofreaders: M'Lou Thompson, Pete Singer

Publisher: Dennis Stovall

Interior Design: Dennis Stovall

Cover Art: Bill Plympton

Cover Design: Marcia Barrentine

Advisors: Ann Chandonnet, Madeline DeFrees, David James Duncan, Katherine Dunn, Jim Hepworth, Ursula K. Le Guin, Lynda Sexson, J. T. Stewart, Alan Twigg, Lyle Weis, Shawn Wong.

Left Bank Books are thematic collections. New books in the series are regularly announced, and author's guidelines may be had by sending a SASE to the series editor.

Pursuit of Happiness is the eighth title in the Left Bank Book series.

First edition, June 1995

Printed in the United States of America on pH-balanced paper.

Contents

Foreword 5

$E = mc^2$ 7
    John Nichols

Dollhouses for Daughters 19
    Lou Masson

Ministry: Homage to Kilauea 25
    Garrett Hongo

Seven Pairs of Women's Gloves and Four
Readings of the Temperature: Following
After Happiness 29
    Lynda Sexson

The Book of the Dead Man (#65) 46
    Marvin Bell

The Government Dog 49
    Gathered and retold by Omar S. Castañeda
    Artwork by Sergio Duarte Méndez

Spirit Tree 77
    Heather Doran Barbieri

Mothers 87
    Nadja Tesich

Hoarse Latitudes 106
    Mark Anthony Jarman

Photos 108
    Jacqueline Moreau

Train Time 111
    Craig Lesley

Expiration Dates 125
    Kari Sharp hill

Fight Club 131
    Chuck Palahniuk

Dreams of Martyrdom 139
    Joanne B. Mulcahy

Fugue in Green 150
    Carolyn Reynolds Miller

Drawing 153
    George Booth

Notes on the authors 155

Foreword

I became intrigued by the idea of happiness for a Left Bank theme after reading Steve Erickson's *Arc d'X*, a novel that time-travels with a Jeffersonian character and explores America's ambivalence about happiness. While we thrive on developing ideologies that aspire to the common good, we stalk hedonist dreams. And yet, "the pursuit of happiness," so long at home in our history, originates from the most noble of instincts — revolt against tyranny. A startling declaration, a radical promise of entitlement to all citizens (or nearly all).

But what does it mean? What constitutes happiness? And how do we pursue it? A Buddhist might call that a contradiction. Can it become an addiction? Can money buy it? Some studies find there is little relation between money and well-being, except for people living in poverty. Ed Diener in the *Psychological Bulletin*, 1984, reports that "during that period [1946–1978] real income in the US rose dramatically (even after taxes and inflation), but there was absolutely no increase in average reports of happiness." He adds that rich people were usually happier than poor people. One can be deceived though, because "the market culture teaches us that money is the source of well-being" writes Robert E. Lane in his article "Does Money Buy Happiness?"

Studies say this and they say that: married people are happier, we may inherit our disposition to unhappiness, women are happier when they have two or three roles, men and women seem to register the same on the happiness scale but women suffer from depression twice as much as men. Prozac helps. Prozac doesn't. Sex does. Sex doesn't.

Even the curmudgeons disagree. Richard Whately, 1787–1863, Archbishop of Dublin, warned that "happiness is no laughing matter." As you'll soon read, Richard Bentall proposes that happiness be classified as a psychiatric disorder. Philip Lopote in his essay "Against Joie de Vivre" said, "Until I have gained what I want from this life, my expressions of gratitude and joy will be restricted to variations of a hunter's alertness. I give thanks to a nip in the air that clarifies the scent. But I think it hypocritical to pretend satisfaction while I am still hungry."

So, in *Pursuit of Happiness* we take up the hunt for that controversial, elusive state of mind and being: happiness.

Here are the random moments of joy as well as measurement by accrual: John Nichols, an early addict to writing, recalls with humor his roller-coaster career; Lou Masson delights in craft and in sharing tools; Garrett Hongo engages in landscape, his familiar Hawaiian terrain; Carolyn Reynolds Miller charts the lusty ground of spring and passion; Jacqueline Moreau's photographs and George Booth's cartoon reward with good humor.

In some stories, hope lies in moving to new territory: Craig Lesley's railroad worker leads his family into increasing isolation as he moves from job to job; Najda Tesich presents Anna who maneuvers between two mothers and two cultures — Yugoslavia on the verge of civil war and the US, her adopted home; the Hmong family who moves to America in Heather Doran Barbieri's piece struggles to stay together.

Other writers court the interior landscape: Marvin Bell gathers force and poise in nonpursuit; Mark Jarman haunts childhood remembrances when contentment seemed easy and safe; Lynda Sexson weaves historical Jefferson with mythical personae in her search for the meaning of happiness.

A few writers explore the dark edges of human encounters, the borderland of addiction: Chuck Palahniuk enters an underworld cult, seeking epiphany through fighting; Keri Sharp hill tackles the definition of love.

And finally, there are the confrontations with the gatekeepers of well-being: Joanne Mulcahy upends Catholic expectations of sacrifice and service; Omar Castañeda's and Sergio Duarte Méndez's graphic myth of a Guatemalan dictatorship brings us full circle to the origins of our Declaration of Independence.

Happiness, we can't promise; spirited, good writing, we can. Enjoy.

— Linny Stovall

John Nichols

$E = MC^2$

Many years ago I reread an autobiographical book by Erskine Caldwell; the name of the tome was *Call it Experience*. In this memoir Caldwell recounted how he'd managed to get his first piece of fiction writing into print. I'm not sure if I have all the facts straight, but as I remember, the story goes like this:

Caldwell sent a whole bunch of stories to Max Perkins at *Scribner's Magazine* and all of the stories were rejected. That got the writer's dander up, and he decided that what was needed was an all out onslaught on that magazine. So Caldwell went up to Maine or Vermont, rented himself a cheap cabin, got in enough wood for the winter, and then he began to type. He wrote one, two, three stories a week, maybe more, and as soon as they were finished he sent them off to *Scribner's*. The magazine poobahs read them, rejected them, and sent them right back. This did not deter Caldwell one whit; he just kept writing stories and sending them off. All through September, October, November, December, January, and February his typing never stopped. He was like a werewolf writer maddened by the moon, determined to succeed. Dozens, then hundreds of short stories wound up in the *Scribner's* mailbox and Caldwell never let up, never got discouraged. He just wouldn't take "no" for an answer. Finally, along about April or May, after this relentless onslaught, he received a letter in the mail from Max Perkins who begged, "Please, stop, no more stories! We're going to publish the last one you sent, on the condition that you never darken our door with a manuscript again." Caldwell shrieked, "Hallelujah!" He promised never to send them another story; he'd finally broken into print. He came out of them thar hills, wrote *God's Little Acre* and *Tobacco Road*, made a million bucks, and lived to a ripe old age venerated by one and all.

My own writing career has been a lot like that. I've always figured bombardment is the name of the game. In fact, I remember in college professors often accused me of employing the "shotgun method" in my exams. I had a peculiar skill, when under stress, of rendering enough orthographically reproduced knowledge during a limited time period to get a high enough grade (exactly 70) to qualify for varsity athletics: I spewed verbiage. I regurgitated words. I set up grandiose smoke screens of palabras. I'm the only person in the history of Hamilton College (a small, liberal arts, all-male school in upstate New York) to turn in eleven blue books, answering just three questions, in a chemistry final exam. And I got a zero on the test.

No matter: I always figured if I sprayed language and ideas in every direction, a few of them were bound to hit a target. Verbal diarrhea was my middle name. The Erskine Caldwell theory of literary success: It's $E = mc^2$. Excess = mass times the energy of typing, squared.

Put another way, I have written about eighty books, beginning when I was knee-high to a grasshopper, and continuing through to the present. And of those eighty books, I've only published fifteen. And here's an update on my condition today: After this wonderful career, I'm fifty-four years old, and in the last six months I almost died of a bout with endocarditis, that blew out the mitral valve in my heart. I married my young and very volatile girlfriend, Miel Castagna. I went on tour for a novel called *Conjugal Bliss* that I just published. I got bogged down with congestive heart failure. I finished writing a script about KayApo Indians in the Amazon jungle for director Ridley Scott while in the Taos hospital. Later, I went into worse congestive heart failure. But I finished a short novel called *Great Feelings of Love* and sent it to my editor in New York, then entered the Albuquerque hospital and had open-heart surgery to repair my destroyed valve. When I toddled out, my editor told me *Great Feelings of Love* was an unredeemable piece of shit and she rejected it cold turkey. So I spent a couple of months rewriting it again while taking flamenco guitar lessons so I could play for my wife, who's a great flamenco dancer, and I also learned how to walk again. My heart went into permanent atrial fibrillation, so I returned to the Albuquerque hospital two weeks ago and got cardioverted by great bangs of electricity back into sinus rhythm. And then last Thursday I began a screenplay of my own novel, *American Blood*, for a producer who just took an option on that book a couple of weeks ago. I'm also writing an article for *Rocky Mountain Magazine* on the forest firefighters who recently died in Glenwood Springs, Colorado. And I'm slated to do a one-week writing workshop in Santa Fe followed by a seven-day photo workshop in Taos, the first two weeks in August. Then I plan to enter that Albuquerque hospital again to get re-cardioverted.

The Ridley Scott project seems to have been shelved; my editor's probably going to reject the newly revised *Great Feelings of Love* novel again; and it's a one in a million chance that *American Blood* will ever reach the silver screen, or that my heart will ever be free of mitral valve prolapse and atrial fibrillation at the same time. But hey, I figure what one of my old football coaches once told me pretty much holds true: As long as you keep moving you're less likely to get hurt. You're also more likely to score. Witness *Forrest Gump*, the quasi-mental retard who's an actual genius, and he *runs*. This is after he's been a college football hero, won the medal of honor in Vietnam, and become a billionaire shrimp salesman. He runs from Maine to California and back, and then back to California again. He doesn't know where he's going or why he's doing it. That's kind of the story of my life.

Yup, much of the time I never knew where I was going, but I sure was a typing fool. And sooner or later, God, the Brooklyn Dodgers, and the Vietnam War notwithstanding, some of it actually worked out.

My first writing teacher was named Miss Cynthia Applewaite. She taught all twelve of us in a one-room schoolhouse in my childhood hometown of Possum Trot, Georgia, population thirty-six. One day when I was in the second grade, shortly before she died of rickets and pellagra, Miss Cynthia gave me a copy of *Finnegan's Wake* to read, and that book really changed my life.

I started writing in the summer of 1955 right after my dad divorced my first stepmother and we, my dad and I, were living in a small apartment in Chevy Chase, Maryland. My dad worked in Washington, DC for the CIA, and everyday I was left alone in our little apartment, so I wrote stories. I wrote them in exact imitation of Damon Runyan, who was my early and most powerful literary hero. My stories were all about New York gangsters and they were written in the first person present tense using very graphic, Yiddish, shtarker slang. For example:

"I'm sitting in Mindy's restaurant on a Saturday night when who should come through the door but Harry the Horse, and he's packing a pizzolaver the size of the Empire State Building. So, before he gets the drop on me, I outs with my own John Rosko and I proceed to practically tattoo my monogram across his chest, leaving him exceptionally deceased indeed."

I wrote my first novel when I was still installed in a remedial English program at the Loomis School in Windsor, Connecticut. Then I went to college and I churned out at least a novel a year, not for any class, not for any grade, not for any professor, just for myself. Writers were considered bohunks and commies back in my adolescence, and you couldn't actually take a course in creative writing because that would have been considered un-American.

One day in college I almost died of blood poisoning, and, during the two weeks I was flat on my back in the infirmary, I wrote a two-hundred page novel called *Don't Be Forlorn*. It was about racism in the South. Another novel I wrote in college was about a blind guitar player called Pheasant Mellow, living in the Storyville Jazz period of New Orleans. His best friend was Jelly Roll Morton. A third book I wrote was about two kids who killed their parents and set up a commune with other kids who've offed their parental units. My point, I think, was to show how evil innocence can be. It was *Lord of the Flies* (long before William Golding thought of the idea) meets *Children of the Corn*. Ultimately, I only managed to show how evil bad *writing* is.

I never could get anyone to actually read my books. Although once, an old professor at Hamilton, to whom I'd given a draft of one of my novels about vegetarian vampires who grow cannibal cabbages at night (using bat shit for fertilizer), showed up in back of my fraternity house on horseback to return the manuscript, unread, and, as he leaned over to hand it to me, he dropped it. The wind caught all the pages and blew them across the campus like leaves from the magnificent maple trees that made shady our bucolic academic haven. That, by the way, is the best distribution of one of my works that I *ever* had.

I graduated, in 1962, from eight years of the best private education money could buy, with no idea of what to do with my life. I thought I'd be a writer, or a rock 'n' roll guitarist, or a cartoonist, or a professional hockey player. I had about as much chance of success at any of those careers as O.J. Simpson has a chance today of being hired for seven figures to plug German cutlery while driving a Hertz rent-a-car through Hell.

One year after my graduation, I found myself living on the corner of West Broadway and Prince Street on the Isle of Manhattan in New York City in a forty-two dollar a month apartment without a telephone, playing my guitar in little coffee houses and dives on Bleeker and MacDougal streets to earn a notoriously meager living and simultaneously writing five novels at once, hoping to strike it rich. One of the novels was called *The Sterile Cuckoo*. It was about a kooky college romance. Another was called *The Wind Heart*, my Scott Fitzgerald book about the disintegration of a robber baron family on the North shore of Long Island. I was also working on a book called *Hey and Boo and Bang*, a chronicle covering the last week in the life of an alcoholic bum who earned a living gathering cardboard in a little cart along the Bowery in New York City. A fourth was a family saga titled *Autumn Beige* about a kid who kills his brother in a shooting accident while they are duck hunting. Another was called the *Wizard of Loneliness*; it dealt with a Vermont family torn asunder by World War II and by an evil nephew who visits them in 1944. But, witnessing the family's agony, the nephew soon becomes a decent and compassionate human being.

Like I said about writing, $E = mc^2$.

The first book I tried to sell was *The Sterile Cuckoo*. I simply took the manuscript up to the offices of Random House or Knopf or Farrar, Straus & Giroux, and I left it at the front desk with the secretary. I included a self-addressed postcard they could send me when the book was rejected, and then I went home. In those days it took about three weeks to be rejected. Then I carted the book to another secretary at another publishing house. I did this about ten times. Occasionally, somebody made a suggestion — one line, just an offhand comment — and I would immediately rewrite the book according to that suggestion because it came from a pro. I would sometimes work twenty-four hours straight without sleep so I could rewrite the book in about six days.

The eleventh publisher, David McKay, said they'd publish it if I could expand it from a novella into a novel. Wow! In about seventy-two hours I added another one hundred pages. David McKay liked them, the book was published, it became a Literary Guild alternate, sold paperbacks for $37,500, and was translated into British, Dutch, Danish, German, Italian, Portuguese, and Japanese. It triggered reviews that compared me to both F. Scott Fitzgerald and Max Schulman, and it went out on film option to Alan Akula (who directed *Sophie's Choice* and *All the President's Men*), and Alan hired me to do the screenplay. I went from earning $500 in 1964 to earning $35,000 in 1965. I spent this money wisely by giving half to a tax lawyer (who took me for a royal ride), by putting my brother through his first year of Dartmouth, by bailing my stepmother out of imminent jail by paying off her debt to the IRS, and by sending my new wife to an orthodontist.

Now, before I sold the novel no agent would touch me with a ten-foot bottle of Perrier. The minute I got money for it, however, agents began falling out of the sky like members of the 82nd Airborne on maneuvers at Camp Lejeune. And the first one that landed at my feet got the job. Thirty years later, we're still together. The agent immediately took my second novel, *The Wizard of Loneliness*, and submitted it to G.P. Putnam, who said that it would win a quarter of a million dollar prize that they were sponsoring. They wined me and dined me at the King Cole Room of the St. Regis Hotel and at the Oak Room of the Plaza Hotel in New York City. They also suggested that I hire a bigtime lawyer to invest all the money I was going to get. So I hired the lawyer, but it turned out the Putnam Prize was

actually a ruse to get distinguished writers to switch their publishers, then nobody won the prize, and that was that.
The Wizard of Loneliness was published. It sank like a stone. It was translated into one foreign language. Guess which one? Polish! Meanwhile, I'd taken a bus to Guatemala to visit a friend and there, totally blown away by the oppression of the indigenous population (thanks to US imperialism), I began my metamorphosis from bright, young talent (and heir to the F. Scott Fitzgerald mantle), to raving Marxist-Leninist, anti-Vietnam war protester and writer of polemical left-wing novels.

My career halted with a screech that was not exactly heard around the world. I never published *Autumn Beige, The Wind Heart,* or *Hey and Boo and Bang*. In fact, for the next seven years I never published anything at all. I wrote five or six or seven novels during that time, but in one way or another they all read like Dobie-Gillis-goes-to-Stalinist-Russia-and-opens-a-tractor-factory-with-Mike-Gold-and-Upton-Sinclair.

I was enmeshed — to the top of my disillusioned, culture-shocked brain — by the struggle between form and content. Fuck form, hail communist content! I mistrusted everything I'd been taught about bourgeois art. I didn't quite come to the conclusion that Chopin was a pig, but I got a lot more out of reading Malcolm X or Ida Tarbell (on the history of Standard Oil) than I did reading the *Alexandria Quartet*. At the same time, I couldn't truly get into socialist realism. Whenever I started writing about a feminist factory worker in Detroit, somehow I'd describe her wearing Brazilian-cut silk panties. Nevertheless, I thought it was probably more valuable to person the barricades than to write namby-pamby fiction that had been inspired by the likes of Truman Capote and W.H. Hudson. So I marched on the Pentagon, organized for peace candidates, read *The Guardian* and *I.F. Stone's Weekly* instead of the *Times Book Review*, and drew anti-Yankee cartoons for Liberation News Service in New York. One novel I wrote was about a guy who goes to Vietnam, wins the medal of honor, comes home, shakes the President's hand, and discovers that America is violent, racist, unequal, crime-ridden, imperialist, and so forth. He winds up venting his disillusion by blowing away his entire family at a cocktail party, then walking down to the seashore and symbolically throwing his medal of honor in the ocean.

Meanwhile, *The Sterile Cuckoo* was made into a decent little movie starring Liza Minnelli, who earned an Academy Award nomination for her work in it. And the theme song, "Come Saturday Morning," sung by the Sandpipers, actually *won* an Academy Award; it was so sappy and so apolitical that I almost committed suicide.

They say that the average writer's public life lasts about as long as that of a marine beachhead commander or a rookie in the NFL. I was twenty-nine years old and I'd already had my fifteen minutes of fame. For some reason though, I kept writing books. I knew they were bad, but I just kept typing. Me and Forrest Gump.

There came a time, however, when it looked like curtains for sure. The year was 1972, the month was November. I hadn't earned a dime in eighteen months. My children were gnawing on the last of the worm-infested turnips that I had carried up from our rootcellar in a blizzard. We were freezing because I hadn't paid the gas bill in four months. I was finally staring into the shiny skull, grinning teeth, and hollow, sunken eye socket reality of "getting a real job," like that of a college professor, or a landscape artist, or a gasoline profusionist.

How did I react to this crisis? Well, I sat down and typed up a novel called *The Milagro Beanfield War* using the shotgun attack, or as my friend Mike Kimmell calls it, the "blam" method of writing. In five weeks I churned out an almost plotless 500 pages with 200 characters. I took three weeks to correct it, three weeks to type it up on my little green Hermes Rocket (the original disposable typewriter), and I sent it to my agent in New York. He sent it to an editor at Holt, Rinehart and Winston, and she bought it for $10,000. The book was published... and sank like a stone. But, thank God, it went out on movie option for the next fourteen years and saved my career. Eventually, it was made into a movie that sank like a stone. Then it was published as a paperback that floated lethargically on the tides of literary reputation, if not popularity, becoming a sort of "cult classic," I believe the phrase is.

I proceeded to publish twelve more books in the next twenty years, none of which probably ever earned back its advance, but a few of which my publisher kept thinking might be the "breakout book" that would justify all their heartache. But none of my books ever broke out, and today, even though nine or ten of them are still in print, the combined royalties in any given year probably don't amount to more than $3,000.

Mostly, Hollywood keeps me alive. My career in movies truly started when I received a phone call at the end of 1979 from a producer asking me if I wanted to meet and discuss a script with a Greek-French director, Costa Gavras, the creator of *Z* and *State of Siege,* among others. I schmoozed with Costa for three days and rewrote a picture that ultimately came to be called *Missing*. It garnered four Academy Award nominations and ultimately won for "best adapted screenplay," but by then I'd been arbitrated out of a credit by my own union, which caused a *very* minor scandal. And I never got to clutch an Oscar in my grubby little fist and shout anti-American slogans over prime time international TV from the podium at the awards ceremony, which is probably just as well.

I did, however, get a reputation as a good guy to hire for liberal, lefty pictures with foreign directors. I speak English, French, and Spanish, and so I proceeded to work on two more pictures with Gavras about nuclear war and science and human values in the Twentieth Century; one picture with Louis Malle about cultural genocide; and one with Czech-British director Karel Reiz, best known in our country for *French Lieutenant's Woman*. And I worked on the film of *Milagro* for Robert Redford. I also spent two years scripting a miniseries for CBS about the life of Pancho Villa and the Mexican Revolution.

Unfortunately, most movies that go through development are never made, and a majority of those movies I worked on never saw the light of day. I published one novel during this time, *American Blood.* It's about the violence underlying our culture. Most people throw it against the wall by page ten and rush to the bathroom and vomit. *American Blood* sank like a stone.

Eventually, in 1988, a bit weary of the film process, I went back to writing novels full-time. I decided to create an epic novel, with about 200 bigger-than-life characters. It dealt with ecological doomsday, environmental holocaust, the collapse of the US banking system, the corruption of our electoral system, the perils of drug abuse and alcoholism, the chicanery of real estate developers, the blasphemous self-aggrandizement of New Age channelizers, and the scandal of no healthcare for the elderly...along with witty ruminations on adultery, male chauvinism, shrill feminism, enterprise zones, leveraged buyouts, golfing, Nazis, raising cats, and so on, for 1500 pages.

After a few years, I finished a draft of this novel and sent it to my editor at Holt. She commonly refers to me as her "favorite, four-foot-tall, Stalinoid dwarf on a soapbox." Let me quote you a few choice lines from her 1990 rejection letter. My book was tentatively titled *Democracy in Action*. My editor wrote, "What's wrong with *Democracy in Action*? After 800-some pages I had to conclude, just about everything. It's got no center and the result is it has no real plot. The scams don't work. The motivations are glossed over, the characters are paper-thin. The effect is part-harangue, part-maudlin commentary, and large-part tedium."

Then, and here's my favorite statement from her rejection: "This is a big monster of an oil spill flowing every-which-way, meaning very little." *Dulce et decorum est pro patria mori*. Well, I sat down and rewrote the book a few more times and it merely became worse. What's the expression — it's just as difficult to write a bad novel as it is to write a good one? You better believe it. I cut that book from 1500 pages to 900 pages. Then I threw out 800 pages and added 250 new pages. Then I switched it from third person to first person. Nothing worked, however.

I finally gave up, sighed deeply, and took a job teaching at the University of New Mexico for spring semester of 1992. It was my first straight job since college graduation in 1962. At the end of the semester I hightailed it back to Taos and wrote a little novel in six weeks called an *Elegy for September*. The story is about a writer with heart problems hunting grouse with an angry, female teeny bopper in the Sangre de Christo mountains, and for some reason my editor bought that and gave me the biggest advance I'd ever received in my life, $40,000 and, of course, it sank like a stone.

Back to the old drawing board.

I have managed to survive, however, with my integrity intact. Some people have commented that in my case, integrity sort of translates as stupidity. Myself, I've always believed that if "you don't get caught up in the geld, you won't get caught up in the guilt." To boot, you may actually live a life that somehow translates down the stretch as an endeavor that was blessed with freedom. Very early on in my career, specifically when I was offered a quarter of a million bucks and then unoffered it in the next breath, I made a decision that whether or not I earned five grand a year or a hundred grand a year, I'd always try to live more or less as if I just had five grand a year, get rid of the rest to good or noble causes or to destitute friends or liquor stores, and that way I could never be trapped into having to do something I didn't want to do in order to pay for my material habits. And life has kind of worked out with a bizarre balance that way. Because I never wanted it much, folks in the art racket have pretty much wound up throwing money in my direction. But I fended it off with the expertise of an antonym to Scrooge McDuck in his money bin, and I never managed to accumulate much of anything that might weigh me down. In fact, I find myself at fifty-four living in a 650-square-foot house, driving a 1980 battered, Dodge truck with 160,000 miles on it, and with three pairs of sneakers in my closet. Coincidentally, I'm also about $80K in debt from a mortgage, college loans, and recent medical fees. But I'm a happy man. Life is a bowl of cherries.

Unfortunately my wife Miel is not exactly a happy woman. Miel thinks I probably had a lobotomy back there a while ago. Because I tend to throw out so many babies with the bath water on my quest for integrity. But I just tell her, mellow out, relax, stick with me kid, and even if the roof leaks and the termites undermine our foundations, it won't matter one whit, because as long as we have each other, we'll just dance down a delightful yellow brick road without a care in the world into a future that is sublime. Whereupon, the charming well-mannered innocent tyke sort of sums up her attitude towards my attitude with a succinct phrase that I suppose might stand as the epigraph to my long and convoluted career. Like, whenever I tell her that the greatest adventures are in the mind, or that integrity means more than moolah, or that material goods don't matter at all compared to the satisfaction garnered from a paragraph written as if the angels of Shakespeare and the devils of Cormac McCarthy were copulating upon my scribbled page, you know what she replies?

"Fuck you, John, and the Olympia portable typewriter you rode in on."

Adapted from his awards banquet address to the Pacific NW Writers Conference, Seattle, July 22, 1994.

Lou Masson

Dollhouses for Daughters

Like my father, I am an infrequent and journeyman carpenter. But I like the feel of a properly balanced hammer, the pressure in my palm from a good plane, and the satisfaction of a task completed. What craft my father possessed he passed to me as I handed him the tools that seemed always just beyond his reach. He taught me their names. I do not clearly remember those lessons, nor do I remember naming the tools for my own children. But the passing has been going on for over forty years. There is a difference, however, between my father and myself: His sons held his tools for him, but I have daughters as well as a son.

I did not grow up with sisters and never watched a father grow with his girls. And I have wondered at odd moments if my father might have grown to be a different sort of man if one of us had been a girl. And I've wondered if I might have been better prepared for my own fatherhood if I had watched my father with a daughter.

For better or for worse, my general fatherly skills are a throwback to my father's approach, or perhaps to the approach of his generation; they are a bit naive and unselfconscious. I suspect the term "parenting" had little currency back then, and even Dr. Spock's bible would have escaped my father. "Gender" and "feminism" and all that these words imply were latent concepts for men like my father. I wish he had lived to see the moments when a daughter has handed me one of his tools. And I wish he could have seen the lives my daughters and I have fashioned together.

My daughters and I built doll's houses. From her books (Mary Poppins in particular) and from old movies, my first daughter had mentally designed a three-story, Victorian mansion that would cost more than we could afford to spend. On several Saturdays in the weeks before Christmas, she and I found ourselves in a dollhouse store comparing the finer points of splendidly miniaturized Victorian homes, the fine furnishings of which seemed as costly as real furniture. True to my middle-class roots, I built what I could not afford to buy. A little girl should have the house of her dreams, I thought, and she should have it as a Christmas surprise.

She didn't. Christmas approached more rapidly than my craftsmanship improved, and the secret surprise house became neither. So on the weekends and evenings just before Christmas I had a helper and foreman to hand me tools, to help with the sanding, and to keep my work as close to her dream blueprint as possible. We measured and planned together. I cannot be certain of her memories but mine hold the remembrance of two people whose perspectives were quite different, trying to see through each other's eyes.

I wasn't thinking about varying perspectives at the time, of course. My daughter and I were concerned first and foremost with bent nails, spilt glue, and missing bits of molding that moments before were right there in front of us. But I have since thought a good deal about perspective.

I have only the vaguest recollections of watching little girls playing with their dollhouses, although I do remember the concentration and seriousness of their play, elements that were foreign to me. I know that all children can focus their attention narrowly when their fantasy world converges with the world we adults call real, and so I expected my daughter's gaze to be directed mostly by her sense of make-believe. But while her imagination did have a lot to do with her vision, I discovered that much more was involved.

We were building a model, I realize now, that was inspired not only by Mary Poppins but also by our family, and by ideal notions of what should go into a house and home that my daughter had abstracted from her brief but alert nine years. She was figuring not only where the miniature furniture would go but the movements of her miniature family. In her overview, she looked through the cutaway back of the house with the eyes of each family member. And her young eyes opened mine.

As the house took shape, both of us would sneak peeks between our working sessions. The cycle of gluing, clamping, and waiting mirrored the frustrations and anticipations of families waiting for real homes to be finished. My skill and ingenuity were tested at every turn: the chimney pots, the tricky staircases, the window moldings. But my daughter never doubted our success. Hers was a confidence peculiar, I believe, to daughters, whose special graces include tolerance, amusement, and patience with a father's work. A man couldn't do much better than work with and for a daughter.

If necessity is the mother of invention, my love fathered a skillfulness beyond my usual talents: It turned out to be a very handsome house. It must have corresponded to my daughter's dream, for she eyed it over and over from every conceivable angle. It measured up. We placed it under the Christmas tree, and it remained there for a week or so. During the holidays I liked to sit in the darkened living room while the rest of the family slept. In the comfortable glow of colored light from the tree, the dollhouse looked real, and I almost regretted the thought of surrendering it to my daughter's room. For it already symbolized something special, and in it I found the telltale touches of its young architect. It was a precocious house of many rooms and staircases, a place of nooks and crannies, a comfortable depository for creative clutter. It was a bold house but slightly old-fashioned. It was, in fact, my daughter.

My daughter took immediate and long possession of her house and kept it in her room long after she was officially too old to indulge in such girlish pastimes. When she left for college, we stored her dollhouse in the cellar, very near the bench where we made it. And when my second daughter was ready for a dollhouse, I proposed that her older sister donate the one in the cellar. No, the old house was to be saved. So life, as it sometimes will, gave me a second chance to build with a daughter.

My second daughter's house was an airy dwelling of few but large rooms, an uncluttered structure of straight lines. She would populate it with figurines of mice and rabbits rather than people. (Each of my architects had her own unique vision.) The cycle of sawing, gluing, and clamping was just as pleasurable the second time, and again I could enjoy working with and for my daughter. Hammers and saws were passed back and forth, and some other tools also. It is hard to name all the tools my generous daughters handed me. With love, without judgment, they taught me to bend down and look through windows and doors that I had never looked through before. With them I discovered rooms, walls, and barriers that I hadn't imagined before. I suppose I came away from our constructions with a newly calibrated tape measure and a sense that I could measure up to expectations in a new way.

When the house was finished we sanded it, and it too found its way under the Christmas tree, and then into her room. It is still in her room, but it's less used now as she approaches that sad season where we reluctantly put away too much of our childhood. Yet she has exhibited a very literal interest in architecture, and she endlessly sketches designs and floor plans. She may design full-scale buildings someday. That may be her trade.

But my trade is teaching literature, and the only dollhouse I encounter is Henrik Ibsen's century-old play, *A Doll's House*. By choice and coincidence it occupies a place in one of my syllabi every year. In his play Ibsen dramatized the life of a woman who suffered from the misunderstanding and misguided love of the two men who should have cherished and understood her best: her father and her husband. Such suffering is an old story; it is also a contemporary story. Ibsen's heroine, Nora, sees herself as a doll daughter and a doll wife whose life has been confined to a doll's house.

This is a cruel and frightening image of confinement, growing as it does from a child's plaything. Yet the father and husband are not evil men. Their cruelty is not obvious or calculated. They were born and bred blind, and Ibsen's play is a way of revealing that blindness. As a dark symbol, Nora's dollhouse is a diagnosis and first step to curing that ingrained and persistent lack of vision. And as I discuss the architecture of the play with my college students, seeing with them its humanity and powerful themes, I watch the young women who know immediately what the play is about and the young men who discover what is at stake. With Nora we all look out from the little windows of comfortable but cruel confinement. I'm not sure if my students know it, but I try to bring to my teaching the new vision my daughters have taught me: that there are different ways of seeing a doll's house.

I wonder what will become of those two miniatures I've helped build. Will they languish in the corner of our cellar? If my daughters have daughters of their own, will the houses be passed to the next generation? Much as I hate to see these abandoned residences gather dust, I would like my daughters to marry men who would want to build dollhouses for their daughters. Or, quite selfishly, I look forward to getting out my old tools and building dollhouses for them myself.

"It is proposed that happiness be classified as a psychiatric disorder and be included in future editions of the major diagnostic manuals under the new names: major affective disorder, pleasant type."

— Richard P. Bentall, Professor of Clinical Psychology, The University of Liverpool. All quotes from "A proposal to classify happiness as a psychiatric disorder," *Journal of Medical Ethics,* 1992, Volume 18, 94–98, are reprinted by permission of the journal and the author.

Garrett Hongo

Ministry: Homage to Kilauea

Thinking about volcanoes gives me hope —
          all the pure of it.
When my two boys were babies, to help them fall asleep in the
          afternoons,
I liked driving them out from the house we always rented in
          Mauna Loa Estates,
up the highway a mile or so through the park entrance,
then plunging down past all the micro-climates and botanical
          realities
until I got to the swing in the road just before the turnout to
          Kilauea observatory at Uwekahuna,
where I could pull over into a little gravel slot by the roadside
     and let all the air-conditioned tour buses
          and shining red rental cars
             and USGS Cherokees and geologists' Broncos
          swoosh by
while I took a long view

over the saddle towards the veldt-like lower slopes of Mauna Loa,
        my boys already asleep in the back seat.
   What I liked was the swoop of land,
the way it rolled out from under my beach-sandaled feet,
     and the swimming air,
          freighted with clouds
     that seemed the land's vision rising over it.
I could have been the land's own dream then,
and I liked thinking of myself that way,
as offspring come to pay it the tribute of my own thoughts,
       little brainy cyclones
that touched down in the lava channels
        or drained back into rivulets of wind.
"Cloud and Man differ not," I joked to myself,
"All is One under Heaven."   And why not?

   What if we were to recast ourselves as descendants
all gathered at the foot of our heresiarch mountains,
drawn by a love like primitive magnetisms and convection currents
     calling all things back to their incarnate sources?
Our lives might be ordered by a conscious abstinence,
a year of giving up to save for a trip home.
We would sacrifice for an earthbound commitment —
         homage to birthplace,
source rock come up from a star's living depth.

What would be the point other than to step into the sulfuric
       cleansing of volcanic clouds?
Our dithyrambs of dream-mountains not quite earth's equal
but more vague than that — like clouds around Mauna Loa,
drifting continents of vapor and dust

riding the gyreing wind-gusts over Halemaumau and Iki,
mantlings of evanescence on the tropical shoulders of an angel?

Aren't we the earth become known to itself,
we celebrants of a sublime not completely dreadful,
but companionable too, its presence like two sleeping children,
innocent dragons
   fogging the car's rear window with a visible breath?

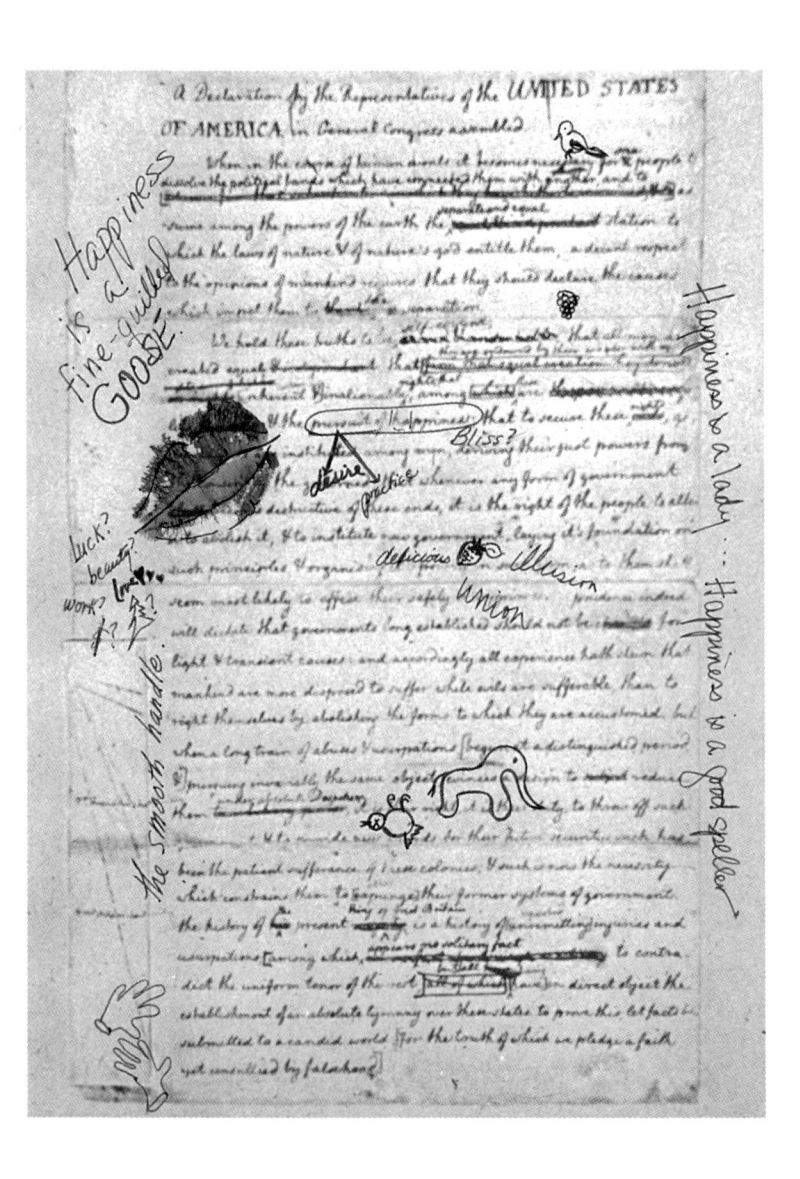

A Declaration by the Representatives of the UNITED STATES OF AMERICA in General Congress assembled.

Happiness is a fine-quilled GOOSE

Happiness is a lady...

luck? beauty? works of? love?

the smooth handle

Bliss?

delicious *Illusion*

Happiness is a good speller

Lynda Sexson

Seven Pairs of Women's Gloves and Four Readings of the Temperature:
Following After Happiness

We American revolutionaries have a guarantee for discontent...*the pursuit of happiness*...It is desire, the chase — not the object — which is guaranteed. The running after.

Not happily ever after.

Ever after happiness.

Deciding to collect on the promise brought forth ten score and nineteen years ago, I pursue the elusive if not illusory word, *happiness*. Did Jefferson declare happiness once the founding fathers had sharpened their quills for their John Hancocks?

> *The only record he left of the day when the Declaration of Independence passed was an entry on the purchase of a*

thermometer and seven pairs of women's gloves, the amount he gave to charity, and four readings of the temperature.[1]
Such an accountant, such a mechanic, such a philanthropist; many pursuits, but happy? The gloves. Did they bring happiness to one woman or to seven?

With the promise of the founders rolled up in my pocket, I search my nation. From Pleasantville to Fairfield, from Happy Valley to Merry Mount, from Harmony to Holiday, at festivals and circuses, I take to the sunny side of every street to inquire after happiness. I hunt down the Town Painted Red with more determination than Coronado seeking the Seven Cities of Gold.

Citizens are eager to help my quest, but point over their shoulders, locating happiness, as Jefferson and Franklin and Adams had decreed, just around the corner. I trace a rumor of a woman devoted to pleasure. First, I ask, as the voluptuary invites me in, is happiness in sensory pleasure? Let me show you, she murmurs.

A bowl of rotting fruit. The woman dumps out the decay and washes the bowl. I love fruit, she says. Though the more I desire, the more I fast.
I pull out the Declaration and begin to make notes on the back. If we cling too hard to life, do we squeeze out happiness? Does the old duplicitous desire for have-your-cake-and-eat-it-too prevent happiness? The anorexic of aestheticians waits…and wastes. *Carpe diem!* I shout.

The raspberry, she says, an astonishing dome constructed row upon row, each drupelet a gush of red juice, each translucent cell surpassing stained saints in church windows. Shall I eat, or shall I look?
The architect of Monticello proposed the temporality, as well as the order and form, of beauty: *The flowers come forth like the belles of the day, have their short reign of beauty and splendor, & retire like them to the more interesting office of reproducing their like. The hyacinths and tulips are off the stage. The Irises are giving place to the Belladonnas…*[2]
Perhaps it was right for Jefferson to cast happiness in the future tense, put it ahead of us so death could not reach out and cast its shadow over it. But did he value purpose and production over beauty?

The woman tries to stretch the pleasure, to save the berries for another daylight. And then in the night the mold takes over and knits the berries together, altering their composition and the woman's desire.

How can I be happy, she asks, given the spoils of time? Even the aloof pleasure of the rampant mold?

She offers me the magnifying glass, so I can see that mold is as formally exquisite as classical architecture. She minds her fruit with regret, but gives me an apple and wishes me luck.

I sit on the step and take of the fruit and eat. And, in honor of Jefferson the horticulturist as well as to the future of happiness, I plant the seeds. Fruit is full of Eros and myth, earth and rot, too intricate a language to embody mere happiness.

Well, if happiness is not in the beautiful, is it in accomplishment, success? Was the eighteenth-century quest for happiness driven by expansionism, a dreadful pleasure entailing the enslavement of Africans at one end of the enterprise and the extermination of Native Americans at the other? Was *happiness* a euphemism for men taking *property*? Surely the old t-shirt that King Midas first wore ("Whoever Dies with the Most Toys Wins") can't be a paraphrase of Jefferson's colonialist optimism. It must be more than the lust for stuff. The Constitution, unlike the Declaration, does not dangle happiness before its citizens. The fifth and fourteenth amendments to the Constitution state that no person shall be deprived of "life, liberty, or property," (keeping in mind that fully participating *persons* included only white males in 1789 and males of any hue by 1868 — women wouldn't have to worry their pretty little heads over these ideals until 1920).

But I keep asking, so folks send me to the richest man on the hill.

A chill hangs around the house. Come in quickly, he says coolly, don't let in the sun.

She ran off, the neighbors whisper, before he could get a good likeness of her, but for that ice portrait. It's easier for a lover to thaw a woman made of ice, they cluck, than for a rich man to enter Heaven. Is happiness a heavenly state? I scribble another note.

He takes me into a dining room, icicles hang among the crystals in the chandeliers, frost coats the silver and silvers the china. A larger-than-life ice sculpture of an odalisque reclines on the table.
The chef had carved it for the engagement party, a centerpiece of the betrothed. But just as the guests arrived, the cook and the model disappeared together into thin air. The rich man searched for her, searched for the chef, pursuing ice sculptures at any price.
I buy and sell ice, by the cube, by the block, by the berg, he says. He rents me mittens and tours me through lockers of ice swans and ice fountains and ice penguins. It would be less costly to keep diamonds, his teeth chatter; and he shows me a room full of them, dazzling as ice. He tours me through a Smithsonian of igloos, ponds of skaters. Icicles are mounted like swords over the empty fireplaces. We stumble over bags of cold cash.
He tends his stocks and flocks and acres and oil and gold, all to amass the wealth of refrigeration, cold air to keep the ice rather than the ice itself, and will someday own even the same thin air into which the beauty and the cook had disappeared. And he will charge by the breath. Inhale and exhale.
I hope she comes back, I tell him.
She did, he says. She deserted the cook and came back. But she was so ardent she was liquidating my fortune, so I froze her out. A woman is less reliable than ice.
Anyone, he tells me, can acquire ice. Only a rich man can keep it. It's not the fickle ice which commands the value, it's the air. He gives me a Popsicle and asks for a dollar.
Money, the neighbors sneer, can't buy happiness. I make a note. But a rational neighbor explains, Happiness can't bring money. I notice the town fool following me, mouthing my questions, mocking the answers.
Jefferson, who bequeathed to the nation the Louisiana Purchase and to his family a mountain of debt, had been too busy plotting a country to tend his own garden. Surely, he couldn't have been thinking of happiness as a word for wealth. Or plunder.
Or even gloves. Spiteful folklore knows him to have slovenly presided in slippers down at the heels, even though he lectured his daugh-

ters on the importance of dress, and even though, on a singular historical moment, thought to purchase women's gloves. Seven pairs. But with all the failings we can pin on Jefferson, we cannot accuse him of mistaking happiness for possessions, of too many gloves.

Perhaps, though, in the engendering of things rather than the accruing of things — in the design of gardens, in the investigation of mounds, in the crafting of a society — there is happiness. The pursuit of happiness may be not in the quest, but in the practice. Maybe work, I note as the town fool balances on a fence.

From the penny-saved-penny-earned school, Jefferson advised his daughter Martha, *A mind always employed is always happy. This is the true secret, the grand recipe, for felicity. The idle are the only wretched.* He put all the grumps on notice that we have a moral obligation to pursue happiness. Only the unimaginative have such corrupt morals as to be unhappy, I annotate the Declaration. As Jefferson said, *Interesting occupations are essential to happiness.*

Near the end of his life, his granddaughter Ellen's wedding gifts, including the hand-carved writing desk he had presented to the couple, were destroyed by fire. Jefferson wrote of the poignant figure of John Hemings who had made the desk: *Everything else seemed as nothing in his eye, and that loss was everything. Virgil could not have been more afflicted had his Aeneid fallen a prey to the flames. I asked him if he could not replace it by making another? No. His eyesight had failed him too much, and his recollection of it was too imperfect.* Does the heartbreak of John Hemings, slave and master-craftsman, give clues regarding happiness? For the sake of the bride? For the sake of the wood? For the skill of the Hemings' woodwork displayed in Monticello or the enlightened eye that gazed upon it?

Jefferson replaced the lost desk with a small writing box *which claims no merit of particular beauty. It is plain, neat, convenient,* but noted wryly, *Its imaginary value will increase with the years, and if he* [Coolidge, her husband] *lives to my age, or another half century, he may see it carried in the procession of our nation's birthday, as the relics of the saints are in those of the church.* Is happiness in a simple item, a wooden companion to fifty years of thinking and writing? *It was made from a drawing of my own, by Ben. Randall* [Randolph], *a cabinet maker in whose house I took my first lodgings on my arrival in Philadelphia in May 1776. And I have used it ever since.* America's altar of independence was Jefferson's modest workhorse for half a century.

As I look at the rosy puddle of my melting Popsicle, I consider, is happiness to be discovered in Jefferson's gift? The writing box meant most to him when he gave it away, with all its accumulated use and meaning, to the wedding couple. Perhaps happiness comes into being only as we give it away, and we feel it pass through us like a breath.

But Jefferson sometimes seemed to reduce happiness to maddening trifles: In 1783, to his daughter, the motherless eleven-year-old Martha whom he called Patsy, Jefferson wrote, *Take care that you never spell a word wrong....It produces great praise to a lady to spell well. I have placed my happiness on seeing you good and accomplished, and no distress which this world can now bring on me could equal that of your disappointing my hopes.* He was himself a various speller.

Happiness is a lady, happiness is a good speller, I note in large letters across the top of America's sacred text. Despite that evidence, happiness won't show up on a report card. But in the eighteenth century, we thought we could calculate it by degrees of pleasure over pain. I visit a tidy house decked with weather vanes and thermometers. A blue bird perches on the picket fence. Must be here, I think I know this bird.

A man with a pencil behind his ear offers me a glass of lemonade. Half full or half empty? he asks politely.

My wife packed her bags, the accountant of happiness confides. All started when we sat down to turkey dinner. Went to say grace, she couldn't count her blessings. Name them one by one, the man had advised his wife, start with me.

She sat there til the mashed potatoes turned to stone. She said I could recite The Ancient Mariner, but hung towels on the doorknobs. I told her that she could bake a cherry pie, but she invited stray cats into the house. It commenced, he said, a great battle between her ledger and mine. We couldn't find a blessing to count without it having drawbacks.

This dilemma causes some philosophers to clap their oppositional hands and recite that goodness requires its absence. The economist of happiness claims scarcity runs the world, that diamonds are beautiful because they are rare, not because they are light catchers.

I may be happier with her absence, her memory over her perfume, he calculates. And now you must leave, he demands, I just cannot figure which side of the ledger to place your question.

Emotional joy is as ephemeral as the Rich & Famous Contract, as incalculable as Peace and Tranquillity. It must be something else that those revolutionaries were after: was happiness another word for liberty? One of (only) five persons granted freedom in Jefferson's will was John Hemings the cabinet maker. His wife was not.[3] Did the slave-owning declarer of independence see a relationship between freedom and happiness? Freedom of thought and happiness? *The rights of conscience we never submitted, we could not submit…..it does me no injury for my neighbour to say there are twenty gods, or no god. It neither picks my pocket nor breaks my leg.*[4] Nothing caused Jefferson more political trouble than his free remarks concerning religion. Then as now, religion was exploited as a political bludgeon; Jefferson's enemies inflamed and distracted by accusing him of atheism. Religious doctrines inhibit social happiness, I mark on my document of freedom. The church had deferred happiness to a contract with the hereafter; Enlightenment thinkers offered the chance to cash in the contract in this world. The terms were still moral virtue, but the rewards were mundane rather than celestial. Yet it was not even the grandest of abstractions — freedom — or religion — or freedom from religion — which made Jefferson sanguine.

Citizens advise me to get out of town, some for making people miserable with this incendiary question, others because, they say, happiness isn't in town, it's in the woods. Maybe so. Taming and tinkering across the new nation which Jefferson helped to stretch across the continent, the founders pursued happiness as land. *Where has Nature spread so rich a mantle? Mountains, forests, rocks and 2 rivers.* American consciousness has never been a match for the glory of the continent. *Sacred and undeniable* as the Declaration of Independence may be, it is a relic of nationalism, and cannot make a planet happy. We need a new manifesto, we need a new Jefferson, to turn from gloves and thermometers, to declare, as self-evident, the rights of the planet to keep forest greening and desert glimmering, the unalienable rights of all species to take their own chances in their pursuit of survival and consciousness. All the moral imperatives for preserving parrots and lady's-slippers are misdirected unless we relocate the impulse not in the ethical, but in the pleasure center. Without happiness, the stones and bones of the planet slip through our distracted fingers. The claims Jefferson took as inherent to the "nature of man," must be reassessed in terms of the nature of nature. I go to the woods, but Jefferson haunts me there, too. And so does the fool, like Jefferson's shade, hiding pencil-thin behind pine trees, his red hair sticking out with the lichen.

What did make Tom Jefferson happy? He told his granddaughter pen pal she had the *great advantage* in letter-writing as she had *a thousand little things which I am fond to hear,* the president of the young United States said he had far less interesting events to report. He told her when to expect him (and ever studious, he sprinkled in a lesson for three Latin terms as he wrote), and *then we will examine the tulips together.* But nature was as utilitarian to the founders as it was to the writers of Genesis; it was there to serve humans. Those cosmogonists of a nation saw that it was good, but also good to eat, and to make them wise. They would own it and harness it. Nature would be a row of tulips.

I take the Declaration out of my pocket and study it. *We hold these truths to be self evident.* Only in the eighteenth century could such abstractions as *truth, life, liberty,* and *happiness* have been self-evident or, as in the original draft, *sacred & undeniable,* and reconciled to their view of Natural Law.

The ink fades on the less-than-timeless parchment. Who can speak of the happiness of the sheep whose skin made the parchment? Having been rolled up and hauled in a wagon, stored in a barn, little wonder there is a crack above the S in States. When the fair copy was displayed in the Patent Office, it faced a window, light streamed in and faded the signatures. When the engraved facsimile was taken in the nineteenth century, chemical deterioration increased. After Pearl Harbor, the Declaration was among the treasures sent to Fort Knox, and the upper right-hand corner was fixed, until it came back to Washington, with scotch tape.[5] Now we watch over our treasure with better light and temperature control. On the day that it passed, our man of measurements recorded the temperature four times. How many of us inheritors of democracy think it is our happiness to help create a climate for happiness for all the citizens? Why am I reading in the woods? Is reading or is solitariness the equation for happiness? I go back to town.

Many of the folks I visit advise me that Jefferson never meant private pleasure, but intended happiness to mean something like the public good. I wonder. Were life and liberty public, and only property private? There are plenty of scholars to suggest that Jefferson meant, primarily or solely, social happiness rather than our contemporary notion of private happiness.[6] We continue to explore privacy — is it domestic life or is it solitary reflection? Jefferson's ideology of family and domesticity are the images which make possible the claim for the public happiness. To Ellen the president wrote, *Your letter of the 11th is received, and is the best letter you have ever written me because it is the longest and fullest of that small news which I have most pleasure in recieving. With great news I am more than surfieted from other quarters.* On the occasion of his second inauguration, he wrote to his granddaughter Ellen, despite *the pressure of the day on which this is written,* and he did not tell his grandchild about riding his horse in the parade, mention any festivity or pomp or significance, only that *I am called off by company therefore God bless you, my dear child,* sending her pieces for her scrapbook. Happiness, I write on the back of the Declaration, is not in ruling nations, but in keeping a scrapbook.

I meet a gang of realists who think happiness beneath contempt. Is a happy person shallow? Stupid? Self-absorbed? I can't blame the pessimists for feeling shame over shabby pleasures, ever since Reagan it's been me, me, me. Or does the blame go back to Jefferson and his cohorts? The notion, though, seems to have narrowed from the sense of a common good and an individual opportunity to simply opportunism. Jefferson read books for the deep happiness of learning and art, to contemplate love; but now we read — if we pursue that pleasure at all — to learn How To Get Someone To Love Me. Jefferson displaced happiness for public service: *But I am tired of a life of contention and of being the personal object for the hatred of every man who hates the present state of things. I long to be among you, when I know nothing but love and delight, and where instead of being chained to a writing table I could be indulged as others are with the blessings of domestic society and pursuits of my own choice.* Is this the writing table that was to become, upon reflection, the gift, the locus of so much happiness? Happiness avoids the present tense, I note.

What makes me happy? I ask. One of the neighbors tell me, you make your own happiness. The neighbor sends me across town to a man and a dog. The neighbors on one side say the man has a heart, on the other side that he is handy. A Jeffersonian. Here I suspect is a man who can pursue happiness.

A stray dog, nose to the ground, finds his doorstep. The man almost trips over the dog's gloomy shadow. He takes in the dog and feeds him toasted cheese, makes him a bed by the fire. He watches the dog's tail for a sign of happiness. The dog turns his long face away from the light. And so the man, moved by his companion's melancholy, builds a machine all clever springs, levers, and switches, returning again and again to the drawing board.
The device resembles Jefferson's polygraph — his duplicating machine with which Jefferson could write with two pens at once — which gave him the pleasurable fantasy of efficiency.

At last he harnesses it to the dog and wires the end of the machine to the end of the dog's tail. This will make you feel good, he says as he snaps the rubber bands and tightens a screw. And now, the man tells the dog, you will wag happily ever after.

The dog, constricted by the robotic tail-wagger, sighs, and I begin to see happiness is not an imposition from external conditions, neither tail-wagger nor fruit nor the all the ice in Antarctica. The dog does not seem happier. Does the man?

Pleasures are fleeting, success is external; happiness, I begin to see is a state of mind. Happiness is not bread & shelter, nor the quality of that bread or shelter, but rather it is in the celebration of them. The condensation of hearth to heart. The man who makes a tail-wagger for a sad dog may fool himself into something near happiness.

But the happiness we make for others is as fleeting as our own.

The dog sees a mouse and the contraption flies apart as he dashes in pursuit. At that moment the dog looks nearly happy. The man is moved to melancholy.

Happiness is as fleeting as sorrow. The fool, his arms too long for his sleeves, his slippers down at the heel, gathers up the pieces of the tail-wagging machine and pokes them in the garden for the morning glories to climb. One November Ellen wrote to her grandfather of their sorrow over the death of her tame Bantam, who flew to her lap and ate from her hand; but by December she wrote disdainfully that Jefferson (the grandson) had gone to see an elephant, *but we did not he was only 7 foot high.* One day we mourn a chicken and the next scorn an elephant. I make a note.

The neighbors tsktsk about one shadowed house. Deciding I have nothing to lose, I visit, but the house is empty. So the gossips lean over the back fence to tell me:

The weight of the diamond rings kept her close to him. The old man died believing the young woman loved him for himself and not his real estate, and the young woman went off with his last testament and the patient heirs gnashed their teeth.

Could the old man have been happy if it was based on delusion? Can the young woman be happy if her joy was sprung from prostitution? The answers, the neighbors regret to say, are yes and yes. Some of us cannot be happy, we protest, if the happiness is evoked by an illusion: an old man's fancy, a young woman's delusion. One of the neighbors shows off a postcard from the glittery girl:

I have a new boyfriend. The dear old goat's dear and handsome nephew. He doesn't care a hoot about the money. He said so.

The neighbors laugh, but no one seems particularly happy.

Among the philosophers who tried to lead Jefferson astray, were Locke, who looked to health and possessions, and Aristotle who sought happiness in virtue, insisting it was linked to the good, though Aristotle's excellent man comes off as a man who would seek a tax break for those with incomes of $200,000. Since the beginning of western philosophy, we have tried to hitch reason and morality to happiness. And, too often, "reason" and "the good" have referred exclusively to patriarchs. Virtue is the kind word for power.

Folks tell me not to give up, to try another man, so happy he never leaves home:

> *It's a hovel, the only running water comes through a hole in the roof, the only food comes from potatoes and turnips in the root cellar. The pleasure, though, comes from a virtual reality game, in which the man lives in a palace, dines upon strawberries and listens to the music of the spheres with wise and amusing companions.*

The neighbors complain, saying the man wastes time and is fooling himself into virtual happiness. Maybe happiness is by definition illusion. We require virtual headgear and gloves — blinders — to persuade ourselves that happiness is possible, with death around the corner and suffering everywhere.

Buddhism, developed two millennia before the Declaration, is grounded in a premise antithetical to the Jeffersonian ideal. The Buddha's first truth is that *all life is suffering*. Not just earthquakes, oil spills, murders, or Ed McMahon never getting here on time with the American Family. All life is suffering because the ego's experience is ephemeral and not real. All is illusion, the great beautiful veil of suffering. And, according to the Buddha's Four Noble Truths, we must detach ourselves from desire. From pursuing happiness. We must live compassionately, but dispassionately. Not easy.

The early Buddhists used to tell a story of a man who, pursued by tigers, falls over a cliff and hangs by a twig. Mad elephants wait for him at the bottom. Drooling tigers above him. Two mice appear and begin to gnaw the twig. The man — deluded by desire — sees a little plant growing in a crevice, and the foolish man reaches for a strawberry. The story was told and retold. In the Zen tradition, we hear the same story, the man clinging to the twig, reaches out and plucks the ripe, red strawberry. Ah, he says, how delicious. In the Zen telling, the man is no longer is trying to save himself, he lives the delicious moment. One story, two views of awakening.

Happiness is illusion — not in the sense of fooling ourselves — but in the sense of fooling. Of play. Illusion is not an imitation of the real thing, but rather that the real thing is inadequate as a paper doll unless it is infused with imagination. Happiness, I mark on the Declaration, is bliss, without content, without me. How delicious. Happiness is a state of consciousness owned neither by the thinker or the thought. It passes through. When it passes through intensely, it is called joy, and permeates all else.

Happiness is just for fairy tales, one sage advises me; etymologically, happy has more to do with luck than effort or virtue. The way of the fairy tale is that the littlest and most foolish one, by good luck — that is by a pure heart receptive to the uncanny — is rewarded with a castle and a princess, and a happily-ever-after. But others warn me over and over, watch out, you may get what you wish for; genies get their kicks from giving the innocent three wishes. Only a fool could be happy, the citizens remind me. And don't, says one bitterly, think happiness is love. When Jefferson wrote nostalgically, playfully, to Ellen, *receive the kiss I give to this paper,* would we discover that happiness is loving someone? What can happiness be, if it is connected to love, and therefore always painful? I blot my lipstick on the Declaration.

There are two sisters with lace at their windows and lace at their throats.
Once, the gossips say, they had suitors to walk them home and eat their pear tarts, full of promise and promises. They tell me themselves what happened.

On the eve of the wedding, one suitor disappears. They drag the river and check the train station and fear the worst for him, says one sister. Think the worst of him, says the other.

The young woman becomes an old one sitting on the porch anticipating his return, never losing hope, the vision of his bright eyes and bony knuckles fresh in her mind. The lucky sister marries the faithful suitor who kept that promise but none other. After he dies, she sits on the porch with her maiden sister, relieved of her bitter times.

Which one of you is the happy one? I ask. The first sister says,

Every child presses a bruise. The other says, all tales are tales of misfortunes. They laugh 'til tears run down their powdered cheeks.

There is a trap: maybe I was happy until I began to ask myself the question. And then the question itself raises doubts, philosophical and psychological difficulties, so happiness slips away. Yet, if I do not question it, I cannot be happy. Happiness seems to imply a self-assessment, an internal affirmation of one's state of being. If I am in the midst of trilliums and streams, with my dog and my lover, and if I am not awake to my condition, I could as easily be in the midst of old aluminum cans and snakes. I know, you can think of plenty of people who despise mountain air or dogs, and plenty of people who enjoy aluminum cans and especially snakes. It's all relative, you say. Yes, but what is not relative is the necessity for self-consciousness. To be happy demands the capacity to reflect on happiness and the greater capacity to leap into that state of consciousness. It seems to have little to do with conditions of the world, no matter what our common sense tells us, it has to do with a perception beyond conditions. I cannot be happy if I don't think about it, I scribble on the Declaration. Then I add, but I cannot be happy if I do.

Can it be in gloves? Seven pairs of women's gloves, fourteen hands, seventy fingers. Or one pair of hands, and the pleasures of them slipping on and off. How happy I am to imagine the gloves — and a woman receiving them, trying them on, perhaps reaching up to Jefferson's red hair, grazing his cheek with fine woolen fingers. Or were they kid, better than the parchment for the Declaration of Independence? Happiness? But gloves were also for mourning, and sent as an elegant form of invitation to a funeral. But even these mourning gloves were marked with the promise — the pursuit of happiness — when they were stamped with a design of the Liberty Tree.[7]

So happiness is even more complicated than all the varieties of love and gloves. I keep referring to the Declaration, perhaps the illusion or reflection of happiness is a disease of literacy. After his granddaughter Cornelia wrote her first letter to him, Jefferson answered, *I rejoice that you have learnt to write for another reason; for, as that is done with a goose quill, you now know the value of a goose, and of course you wil assist Ellen in taking care of the half dozen very fine grey geese which I shall send by Davy.*

I write in large letters, Happiness is to know personally, to feed, to admire, and to kill, pluck, and pare your own pen. Happiness is a fine-quilled goose.

Too complex, geese and writing. I decide to make it simpler:
   Red.
   Red is happy.

Not a red dress, red blood, a red tulip in Monticello's gardens, nor the red apple the woman gave me, nor the red Popsicle from the ice man. Not the town painted red. Not even my son's red hair. Not the red hair of the fool who keeps pestering me as I search for happiness. Not even the Zen strawberry. Not the crimson dress, *with the tail like a 'robe de cour,'* that Martha Jefferson wore to the fashionable school in Paris, nor even her red hair, nor her Papa's. *We have indeed an innate sense of what we call beautiful, but that is exercised chiefly on subjects addressed to the fancy, whether through the eye in visible forms, as landscape, animal figure, dress, drapery, architecture, the composition of colors.*
   Just red.

I think it makes me happy. (Although, as I continue to search for happiness, I meet a man so angry he sees red; and I pass by a woman in a red shirt relentlessly pursued by hummingbirds.) But as close as I come is to hear of someone tickled pink. By the time I reach him, the chameleon is blue again, watching old movies and weeping. His wife says to weep over *La Strada* makes him happy.

If happiness is the word for the taste of a plum when bowered by the yielding plum tree, for the scent of a man fresh from labor, for the sound of a wolf howling, for the touch of a rabbit, for the sight of a crinkly face, then happiness is limited by time and death, by the rot of the fruit. Would pleasure without boundaries, life without death, evoke unhappiness as surely as transitoriness? *My only object in life is to see yourself and your sister, and those deservedly dear to you, not only happy, but in no danger of becoming unhappy.* What sort of happiness would that be? Jefferson's big-hearted gift was contingent upon the fire, the loss of Hemings' work, the distance from his beloved grandchild, the end of his own life. He gave them the writing box, not only because it was to be a relic, but, I suspect, because he knew he was about to join the saints of the religion called America.

Just red. But, even a simple red crayon tells too much, makes us feel too much, recall too much. Does the intensity of any pleasure turn it inside out? Is love always bittersweet? Chocolate begins to gag us, swimming eventually prunes us — we've got to come out of the water. A story has to end. Happiness is not in the water or out of it, not continuation, but it is in the variation, the rhythm, swim, shower, drink water, lie down in the dark, make love, sleep, dream, wake up to light and crows. A story is in the rhythms of knowing and not-knowing, of pain and pleasure, beginning and end. Happiness is not the ego's pleasure, but the planet's rhythms.

I cannot hold to red very long without thinking red dress or red blood or red apple or red hair. And then, the pleasure is submerged into something more tangled, more perplexing, the mix of consciousness. Sensory perception, after all, is interpretation, cognition. There is no experience of red without context, without light and shadow, time passing, and thought.

Is happiness the knowing of it? It is not red, but the knowing of red. The joys of reflection: *Then we will examine the tulips together.* Surely happiness is not just the distraction between pain and oblivion, desire and death. Happiness may be the faint call from a state of awareness the mystics know.

The gangly redhead follows me, from the woods to the town, keeping his distance but also his interest. I ignore him, despite his mournful look. Pay no mind to that old fool, the neighbors say. I reach in my pocket, the Declaration is gone. I turn around, and there is the fool, slippers down at the heels,

You dropped this, granddaughter, he says. He rolls it tighter, and gives it a kiss. What is it, I whisper. What is happiness? I'm just passing through, he laughs and hands me the rolled-up promise. Wait. What makes you happy? Because you ask, he calls, disappearing.

We told you, the gossips complain, he's a fool, always chasing after butterflies.

In all the world I thought there was only one philosopher of happiness. Jefferson didn't know him: it was Chuang Tzu, who found government foolish, but found foolishness to be bliss. He was the man who dreamed he was a butterfly and ever after wondered if Chuang Tzu the man might be a butterfly's dream. The closest Jefferson ever came to that Chinese sense of free and easy wandering is found in the least likely place, in a pious and practical decalogue he composed for his grandson, the ninth rule is: *Take things always by their smooth handle.* The easy, the gentle, the old Taoist philosophers said. Maybe Jefferson did know them. Happiness, the smooth handle.

Receive the kiss I give to this paper.

---

[1] Garry Wills, *Inventing America: Jefferson's Declaration of Independence.* Garden City, NY: Doubleday & Company, Inc., 1978, 119.

[2] All of the quotations from Jefferson's letters can be found in *The Family Letters of Thomas Jefferson,* Edwin Morris Betts and James Adam Bear, Jr., ed. Columbia: University of Missouri Press, 1966.

[3] Paul Finkelman, "Jefferson and Slavery: 'Treason Against the Hope of the World'," in *Jeffersonian Legacies.* ed. Peter S. Onuf. Charlottesville: University Press of Virginia, 1993, 206. John Hemings' wife lived with him, and was owned by Jefferson's daughter.

[4] Thomas Jefferson, *Notes on the State of Virginia.* Chapel Hill: The University of North Carolina Press, 1955, 159.

[5] David C Mearns, *The Declaration of Independence: The Story of a Parchment.* Washington: The Library of Congress, 1950.

[6] See Wills, 164 and elsewhere. See Jan Lewis on the way in which "public" and "private" derive their meaning from each other in, "'The Blessings of Domestic Society': Thomas Jefferson's Family and the Transformation of American Politics," 111, in *Jeffersonian Legacies.*

[7] Alice Morse Earle, *Costume of Colonial Times.* New York: Charles Scribner's Sons, 1894, 116–7; 1888.

Marvin Bell

The Book of the Dead Man (#65)

1. About the Dead Man's Further Happiness

If truth begins in heresy, then the dead man's capacity is the root cause.

If the future is famished, if every angel is terrible, then the dead man's appetite is to blame.

Tuber or bulb, grit or grub — the dead man is not above a bit the amalgamate malarkey of the underworld.

To the dead man, the abyss is not the pit it was said to be, but is elsewise and otherwise.

The dead man's refusal to mourn is notorious, gladly has he traveled in stateless realms: child of a universal Diaspora.

The dead man's shoes are too muddy, too shabby, to have been left to chance.

Do not assume, what with his high jinks and horseplay, that the dead man has not sometimes had the smile wiped from his face (Mister).

He, too, has been made to wish he was someone or somewhere else.

He, too, has been told to suffer in silence.

Yet he has flourished under the gun, been free in his chains, ducked and sidestepped his captors without moving.

To the dead man in solitary, alone with his thoughts, the world was two things at once.
Why is he, root cause and effect, happy and was he?
And why was he happy — and is he?
The dead man confounds the carriers of salt water who hang about looking for open wounds.
He misleads the bullies, the roughriders, the toughs and the thugs, he defuses, he disengages, he acquits, discharges and absolves.
The dead man's behavior befits the nearly departed, the temporarily indisposed, the tailored by-product of our declination — here and gone in a jiffy, in a twinkling, in a flash.
Ah bliss, that fairly glories in the grave and the ephemeral.
Ah sensible gladness, that reflects equally the divisible and the divine.
For it is the dead man who recalls the sea to the shoreline where sandpipers print the beach.
And it is the dead man who summons from the ocean floor the clay to make the stone egg that safeguards the fossil.
For the dead man's rogue ruminations get under his skin, he worries and pleases himself equally — parent and child.
Yet his unhappiness was turned round as if it had met a wall and could go no further.
The dead man in his earthly joy has taken transcendence down a peg.

2. More About the Dead Man's Further Happiness

That he wanted to be there and not there was to him to feel desire doubly.
That he wished twice as hard was to him to manifest a method to his madness.
The dead man must be doubly peaceful to know peace.

He must be twice as ecstatic to fathom himself orgasmic.

He must be two times the man he was, twin to a twin, a voice congruent with its echo — twice cursed, twice blessed.

The dead man sees the armored crab take to the bait.

He smiles to see the bait take the crab and the tide turn tail.

He hears the slatted sides of his craft complaining to the waves.

He laughs to hear the salt water wearing away its knuckles.

The dead man risks the peril of your affection for a laugh that is also a yawp and a howl, and the hail that is also farewell.

Where there is no second sight, no reconsideration, no disconnection of wishes granted from dreams deferred, then okay good sense is sensory and grief a wispy exhalation of melancholia.

He who became the dead man was made to feel doubly: active and detached, refreshed and depleted.

The dead man's ups-and-downs are to him private peaks and valleys measured by their distance from the moon.

The Government Dog

Based on a folktale of the Tzutujil-Maya of Guatemala

Gathered and retold by
Omar S. Castañeda

Artwork by
Sergio Duarte Méndez

INTRODUCTION

The following story is a folktale gathered in Santiago Atitlán in Guatemala. All effort has been made to be faithful to the original and yet to make the work more understandable to American readers.

Guatemalan Maya folklore is interesting not only for its blend of the traditional with the contemporary, in obvious terms of mixing earlier figures with present sociopolitical realities, but also in subtler conjoinings that point to stylistic tendencies that transcend folklore. For instance, the joining of audience and narrator into what has been called "performance" is found in documents ranging from land surveys to Guatemala's great work of literature, the Popol Vuh. *The relationship between teller and audience is more intimate than American readers generally are used to, and it is one based on collaboration in the narrative act. A "work" is greatly diminished without the smooth integration of spontaneous elements in the audience and narrator interaction.*

Time, too, is an extraordinarily important aspect of traditional Maya culture. The Maya have been very sophisticated in their codifying and partitioning of time while simultaneously blurring divisions of simple past, present, and future, or simple historical time and mythical time. For western readers, these shifts and meldings can seem to be mere confusion. They are not. The manipulation of time is, at the very least, an aesthetic element. One consequence of this technique is that it encourages greater reader participation in constructing events. Another consequence is that symbols are borrowed and then developed across these temporal zones.

And, as with folklore everywhere, there are formulaic aspects in the style: most visible here in the repetition of certain words or phrases and in the use of couplets, triplets, and variations on the two combined.

The folktale was gathered under a Central American Research Award from the Fulbright Commission during the summer of 1989. The artwork was made over a ten year period and independently of the text, yet we hope the two complement and illuminate each other.

THE GOVERNMENT DOG

Between the volcanoes of San Pedro and San Lucas, beside the crystalline waters of Lake Atitlán, there once were nights iridescent with lights, days filled with warm chatter. There once were wizards known as naguales.

They are coming back, it is said. They are on their way here. They are coming now.

Listen, long ago, long ago, O, I can't tell you how long ago, the naguales were here. They were wondrous shamans, magicians with knowledge of things we cannot even imagine. Just as you, with your wide eyes, can see those uniformed men, their machetes and long black rifles, O, the naguales saw inside the hearts and minds of people. They helped with the sowing and harvesting of corn. They helped with lamentations and beseechings. They spoke to our forefathers.

Long ago, they were here. But now they are gone.

Listen — never mind those men — I will tell you something. Before — listen! — before, when the people of Santiago took to the highways to sell *pitaya* and avocado, there came the government dog. He was terrible. He gripped cigars in his teeth and drank rum. He walked across the plaza on his hind legs, and he wore bright silver armor, this dog of the government.

Back then, our men went to Mazate carrying nets plumped with fruits. They went to Mazate and labored with people from all over the country. In those days, I can tell you, Tzutujil and K'iche, Kanjobal and Mam, Ixil and Kekchí sat side by side. The air rang with the marimba, the ground brightened with flowers. There, between this sky and this earth, we, the natives of Guatemala, spilled free our goods.

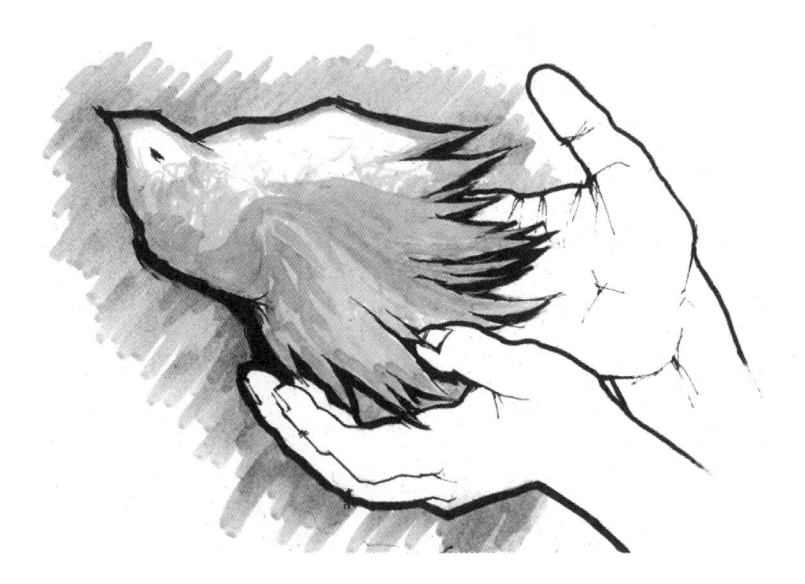

But the dog was ferocious.

"You go down there to Mazate," the government whispered to their dog. "Go down to the great hall where the Tzutujil sleep."

So the dog, long and black, loped toward Mazate. His teeth gnashed under the moonlight. His paws rumbled across the mountainside to arrive at Mazate.

They were just sleeping in the room, sleeping like children, the men of Santiago. Just peaceful and quiet under a pale lunar blue.

That dog slipped into the room with his cigar burning hot. He crept across the room like a finger of a shadow and touched his ember to the feet of those men.

"Our men aren't coming back," cried the women of Santiago. "They are vanishing in Mazatenango!"

The children waited, too. "Where are our fathers?" they called out.

But the husbands and fathers never returned.

GUATEMALA :
83500 asesinatos desde la intervencion yanqui en 1954

The dog was a demon. He could speak Human and Bird and Horse, and he told the horses of the government, "Take these bodies. Deliver them to the capital." Those horses whipped up the night with their tails. "Take this meat to the capital," the dog ordered. "Go!" The stirrups cracked and clattered as they galloped off.

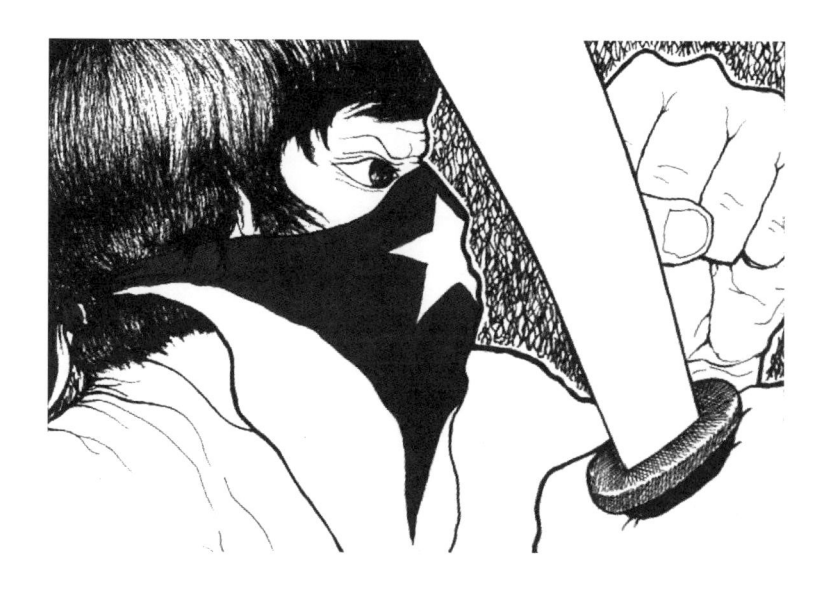

"We are missing our brothers, our fathers," said the people to the naguales. "Our husbands do not return from Mazate. Where are our sons once they leave for market? Where are our grandfathers? Tell us that."

"Okay," said the naguales. "We'll just look into this. We'll see what is happening."

So, they brought out the crystals and the *Tzite* beans. They counted out the days of the calendar and read the prophecies of each day.

"This dog is really tremendous," they said to one another. "He is very strong."

"Just killing is what he loves."

"Just stealing the life of people."

The naguales explained to the Tzutujiles, "We will go and take a look, there in Mazatenango. Wait for us. We will return."

They went like ordinary men. They carried *túna* and avocado in their tumplines. They spread out blankets and joined with others in the market. They talked with everyone they met. Later, they opened their mouths and yawned behind their hands. They said, "My sisters, my brothers, we really must sleep."

And when the room became quiet there in Mazate, a black shadow inched its way in.

"Ouch!" screamed a nagual.

"Hey!" screamed another.

Their feet were on fire.

The dog was tremendous. They could not kill it with machetes. Stones bounced off its armor. They could not kill it with bullets. The naguales used magic and the sky erupted in colors. Yet that dog was too strong, that dog with the long black snout.

"We shall see what to do," the naguales said to one another. "We'll look just a little bit more into those crystals and beans. We'll divine just a little bit more about what we should do."

So, the naguales counted the days again, and they burned *copal*.

They returned to Mazate, these twelve naguales. They went with sandals and short pants. They went carrying only stones with faces, only the names of their ancestors inside their hearts.

"We have come," they said in Mazate.
"And now you can leave," the dog snapped back.

They fought with machetes, with knives and sticks. The skin of the beast was like armor. Nothing would finish him, nothing would kill that government dog.

"Just fly up," one nagual shouted. "Fly to the middle of heaven."

One became a quetzal and flew high into the sky. Another had a stone inside his pocket. It was a small stone, like a seed or a nut, which he pulled from his pocket. The others fought hard against that dog, but it would not die. Nothing would stop it.

So, the nagual threw the stone and it grew and grew until it became enormous — as large as Lake Atitlán, nestled among the volcanoes, glimmering under the sun, brightening there at the center of all of Guatemala. Then the quetzal dove down and grabbed the dog — teeth tearing, paws scratching empty air, jaws snapping at wind.

When that dog fell, the mountain peaks trembled. His flesh thundered like metal. The swords of his paws shattered, and the helmet of his head cracked wide open.

"Now!" said the naguales to the horses. "Take this to your masters. Let them eat this meat in the United States!"

They slapped the rumps of the horses and watched the dust lift up from the road.

In the capital, the government worried. "Find out who killed our dog. Find out who did this. He must be very powerful. We must know the truth!"

Yet the naguales already walked the paths and avenues of the countryside. Like old men, like ordinary people, like women going down the road, they came back here.

"Send our army to ask them questions. Find out the truth!"
But the people didn't know.
"We were just working our fields, just eating our beans. We don't know who killed your dog. We are just living here, peacefully, just praying and singing."

"Tell us!" the army said.

The army questioned everyone. They opened houses, but no answer came. They forced people into the streets, but nothing was discovered, no word extracted.

"Then we will stay until we find out."

"But we don't know anything!" everyone protested.

Yet their mind was set. "We will stay until we find out what it is you do know."

The people shook their heads.

"Then this is what we will tell you: That person is tremendous who killed your dog. Who knows when he may return?"

"It has been shown that happy people, in comparison with people who are miserable or depressed, are impaired when retrieving negative events from long-term memory."

— Richard P. Bentall

Heather Doran Barbieri

Spirit Tree

My son is a vanishing boy. Every time we track him to some condemned building, he slips away, a feral animal of the night. We only hear from him if he's in trouble, a casual phone call, as though we'd just spoken to him yesterday.

"Hi, Maa," he says.

"Liu, where have you been? We've been worried about you. When you didn't come home…"

"I'm in juvi."

"What?"

"Juvenile detention. Jail for kids."

"I don't understand. What happened?"

"They think me and the guys have been dealing."

"Dealing what?"

"Drugs, Maa."

I lean against the wall. The rippled texture of the paint presses into my skin.

"You there, Maa?"

"Is it true?" I sigh.

I already know the answer, know the excuses he will make with his swift, silver tongue, each lie formed so prettily with his lips.

"It's all right. The cops don't have anything on us. Could you come and get me? They won't let me go unless my parents show up. They want to make sure I have somewhere to go. You know how it is."

Yes, I know how it is.

My husband and I take the bus down to get him. I grasp my husband's arm, because if I don't, I might drift away on a river of neon and exhaust and noise. Finally, the bus doors groan open and spit us out in front of the detention hall.

My husband stands in front of the desk, his chin stuck forward with what remains of his Hmong pride. "We are the parents of Liu Xe."

The woman peers at him over her glasses. Her hair spikes from her head like a golden cockatoo. "I'm sorry. I can't understand you."

"Liu Xe. He is here, yes?"

"How do you spell that?"

"L-I-U-"

"Wait a minute. L-E-"

"No, L-I-U," My husband repeats slowly. "X-E."

"S-E-"

"No. X-E."

"Whatever," she shrugs her shoulders and shuffles the papers.

My husband taps the counter with the torn stub of his bus ticket, The sound annoys her. She takes a deep breath. "Wait here."

She goes through a smoke-glassed door, relieved to make us somebody else's problem.

A man, tall and pale as a rattan tree, appears and escorts us down a long, dimly lit hall.

"You know," he bends toward us, "if he's brought here again, it'll be a mandatory two weeks."

My husband nods his head rapidly, a fisherbird gulping water.

"All right, just so you know," the man says. "I'll be right back."

We sit in the cold, green room for some minutes before the guards bring Liu to us.

My husband looks at our son long and hard.

I stare at the floor, tears rimming my eyes.

"How could you do this to your family?" my husband says through clenched black panther teeth.

"We traded opium all the time in Laos, Daa," Liu shrugs. "What's the big deal? I'll be more careful next time. Here you just have to keep from getting caught."

"It's not the same thing at all. We're in the United States now, We don't grow our own maize or millet or hemp or poppies. There is no land for us here. There is no trading like that here. Look at you. You're turning into a crook, selling these bad drugs that have nothing to do with the Hmong way. You have forgotten who you are."

My husband presses his lips together. He won't speak again that night. The shame eats at him like locusts. He remains this way, his rage wrapped tight inside, all the way home on the bus.

I pull my *pandau* from my bag and stitch through the silence, expressing loss through craft.

Liu shifts in his seat, not meeting our eyes. The steel-blue vinyl upholstery squeaks and groans from his fidgeting. He flattens his nose against the fogged window and bangs his hands on the glass. He raises two fingers in a signal to his bad friends who loiter outside somewhere, beyond the wall of steam. Since I've last seen my son, he's tattooed his fingers with strange markings, a secret language I don't understand.

When we get off the bus, Liu has the sense to walk behind my husband. I follow, my eyes on the two stocky silhouettes, so similar in form, so different in mind. We pass the park, where happy families play on slides and swings, the community center where the Tibetans celebrated their New Year, the cafe filled with conversation and clinking cups. And as we walk by, I imagine heads turning and tongues clicking, as if everyone knows our shame.

Like my mother who shakes her head as Liu slinks past her wordlessly and shuts himself in his room.

He turns on the radio, blaring heavy metal music through the apartment.

"He has no respect for his elders, for his ancestors," she purses her lips like a wise meercat.

My husband ignores her and goes outside onto the balcony to smoke a cigarette, his movements stiff and controlled. The metallic scrape of blade on blade mingles with Liu's music as my husband sits in the darkness and cleans and sharpens his knives and pruning tools, knowing the curves of steel so well that he needs no light.

I stand in the middle of our apartment, feeling the walls coming apart, my arms hanging limply at my sides, the muscle separating from bone.

The following morning, I find Liu's bed sadly smooth, no imprint of his body on its sheets.

In the next room, my mother's bed is already empty. She has taken it upon herself to pray for Liu's return. She keeps vigil at the neighbor's plum tree, the same tree my husband prunes twice a year, the same home where he tends the garden. My mother's presence there embarrasses me. But I don't dare say anything to her, because she'll accuse me of being shamed by my own heritage. She believes the spirits have decorated the tree with paper streamers, a sign of blessing on us, on our coming to the new country. A sign that if she prays long and hard enough, Liu will come home to us and be the sweet boy we remembered in Laos.

I don't have the heart to tell her that the sacred ornaments are only toilet paper, thrown through the branches not by good spirits, but by teenagers, including her other grandson, Vang. Soon the paper will disintegrate in the rain, and the kids will find another tree to t.p.

"Did you have anything to do with that?" I ask Vang.

"With what?" He slumps onto the couch, his feet on the coffee table, watching television.

I move his feet off the table.

"You know what I mean."

He shrugs, slouched down into the bulk of his letterman's jacket. He is a standout soccer player, a straight-A student, plenty of friends. A real American kid.

All of us have learned the American ways, pooled our money for the rent on the apartment, started a landscaping business, learned English. All of us except for my mother.

"The toilet paper on the McCauley's tree."

"It was just a joke. Everybody does it."

"You embarrass us. We're their gardeners. They expect better. I want you to go over there and clean it up."

"Aw, c'mon," he groans.

"You know what the worst thing is?"

"No, but I have a feeling you're going to tell me."

"Your grandmother thinks it's a spirit tree."

"You're kidding!" he laughs.

"It's not funny. It's sad. Besides, it's raining. It will all turn to mush, and she'll think it's a bad omen."

"She'll be okay. There will be plenty more where that came from, whether I have anything to do with it or not."

I glare at him. Smart boy. The words of my mother echo in my ears: "*Koj tsis cob menyam,*" she says, you don't teach your children to obey.

I march into the kitchen and scrub the pots in the sink furiously. Their aluminum bodies clang my displeasure. There is no movement in the other room to indicate that he's heard me or that he cares. Complete silence until the phone rings. Then I hear the squeak of couch springs as he shifts his weight and picks up the receiver.

"Hey, man, what's up?"

Probably one of his many friends. Friends that know nothing of his life in Laos. I wonder what they would think if they knew. I wonder if Vang even thinks about it much now. Our life there seems very far away. Like Laos is on another planet, not an ocean apart.

I think of how my sons ran through the jungles there, catching snakes and frogs in the elephant grass, how they hunted pheasant with their father, how they'd been such good fighters against the communists, boys a mother could be proud of.

When the North Vietnamese Army tried to take our village, my sons stood at their post, manning a machine gun. They didn't move, didn't fire until the soldiers came spilling out of their tanks like ants from a burning anthill. They dug their heels into the earth, leaned back and fired the gun, their bodies jerking violently from the vibration. The soldiers, all of them older, more well-trained, dressed in new boots and uniforms, fell before them, these young skinny boys in tattered clothing.

One is the boy I never see — he runs with a street gang. The other wears a letterman's jacket and talks back to his mother.

The side door opens. My mother has finally come in from the rain.

"Ai, this is bad, very bad," she mutters to herself.

"What is it, Maa"?" I ask.

"*Us dab taub dab qhev!*"

"What do you mean you'll be a slave of the demons?"

"The spirit tree." Tears form in her eyes. "The demons sent rain and wind to destroy it."

"It will be all right."

"That's what you always say. You forget Hmong ways. You forget the spirits and your ancestors."

"Do you have any idea how hard this is for me?"

But she has already left the room. She pads down the hall in her damp hemp sandals. The door to her room closes with a quiet, final clap. She will rest on her bed, her arms crossed over her chest, eyes closed. She might refuse to eat or speak for days.

"Vang, get off the phone, please." I call.

He pretends not to hear me.

"Now!"

He groans. "Gotta go. I'll call you later, okay? Now that Liu's gone, she's always on my case. You know how it is. Bye."

"Come here."

He slouches against the wall, arms folded.

"Your grandmother just came home."

"Yeah?"

"She's so upset about the spirit tree that she's shut herself up in her room."

"She always does that," he shrugs. "She'll get over it."

I look out the kitchen window. I clench my teeth so tight, they could break. My face grows hot from the steam that rises from the dishes and the anger and helplessness that rush along my veins.

Then I notice the branches of the witch hazel tree in the courtyard. They reach toward the sky, beaded with necklaces of raindrops. This time of year the witch hazel has a few figlike leaves. A couple of months from now, in winter, it will bloom with yellow, spiderlike flowers that have a subtle, entrancing fragrance. A scent people will notice only after they have passed by. They will retrace their foot-

steps, trying to find the spot where it first affected them.
As I stare at the tree, an idea begins to form itself in my mind.
"There's something I want you to do," I turn toward my son.

The next morning, I tap gently on my mother's door. There is no answer. "*Kuv tus niam,* my mother, come look outside," I call. "We have had visitors during the night."
I push open the door. The shades are drawn. She lies on her back on the mattress and keeps her eyes closed as though she doesn't hear me. But I can see her eyelids twitching as she struggles to remain unnaturally still.
"I know you can hear me...."
I stand near the ancestor altar she has set up in the corner of the room, decorated with pictures of our deceased relatives and incense sticks and a bowl of rice, because she believes we must not let them go hungry, or they will make our lives difficult on earth.
"You know the old saying," my mother sighs, "*Qhiav laus ahiav tsis ntsim. Neeg laus neeg tsis tij lim.* Old ginger isn't peppery; old people have no energy.... Maybe today my time comes. Maybe today I die."
"Please," I smile so hard and dutifully that it hurts my cheeks. "I have important news. The spirits have found a new tree — the one outside our window."
She opens one eye and gives me a sharp look. "You trying to fool an old woman?"
"No, you have seen more stars than I have," I say respectfully. "*Hauv mis koj xub noj. Hauv tsoos koj sub hnav.* You drank at the nipple and wore clothing before I did."
"So you haven't forgotten all the Hmong proverbs, eh?" A smile touches the corners of her lips like the edge of a skirt lifting in bitter wind. "You're just trying to get on my good side."
"Will you come?" I ask politely.
"Well," she says suspiciously. "All right. But you'd better not be fooling me."
She pulls on her purple raincoat. The pointy hood gives her the appearance of an impish wood spirit. Then she fills her bamboo bas-

ket with offerings — tarnished French piaster coins, incense, old chicken bones.

"Here," she says, offering me a cloak the color of green moss. "A sweater isn't enough in this weather. You'll catch cold."

She likes to fuss over me now and then, her youngest daughter. She still thinks of me as her *menyuam mos liab*, her little parrot, her child. Now, she takes my arm to steady herself as we walk down the faded scarlet stairs and into the morning. A thick fog, like spun wool, wraps us in its smoky blanket, making the landscape more mysterious.

"*Auj!*" My mother exclaims. She drops her bamboo basket and presses her hands to her cheeks. "They have come. It is so beautiful."

My son has done his job well. Crepe paper, colored purple, pink, and blue, rustles in the breeze. Strands of clear plastic beads catch what light there is and transform the cheap, dime store jewelry into a treasure chest of precious gems — diamonds, emeralds, sapphires, topaz.

My mother takes my hand. Her fingers are gnarled ginger roots. Her palms are toughened from a lifetime of calluses like an aging panther's paw.

"Come, daughter, pray with me," she whispers.

We kneel in the grass. Dew soaks our legs.

My mother sings, her voice thin and sharp as a snow owl. "O, spirits of the homeland, fly across the great waters, find us here among the changes, the naked trees, the cold rains, the vast concrete city, the people who do not know the Hmong way. We remember our ancestors. We remember the fields of red poppy, the ripe grains of maize, the limestone mountains. We honor you. We will not forget...."

She gazes at the paper streamers on the witch hazel tree, her eyes clear, believing. She squeezes my hand, drawing me into the magic.

"Throw the buffalo horns with me," she says.

She clicks the pieces together several times. They are old. My grandmother, a shaman, had given them to her. They had been handed down from our ancestors, generation to generation for centuries, two halves of a single buffalo horn, representing the worlds of yin and yang.

My mother tosses the horns, chanting, "Mother and Father Kuam, what is the reason for this sickness in our family? Do you require a cure?"

She bends down and studies the pattern the fallen horns have formed.

"Hmm," she murmurs. "Just as I thought. The ancestors feel that we have forgotten them. We must perform a sacrifice to appease them."

She sets out a plate of rice and meat and burns sticks of incense.

"I will do this every morning and every evening," she vows. "You will see. The ancestors will help us. Liu will find his way home."

I close my eyes and my mother carries me back over the fields of Laos on wings of song. There, along a path far below, I see my lost son riding a water buffalo. His sandals dangle from the beast's horns.

I call to him. "Liu, Liu, I'm up here!"

But he doesn't hear me. He swats at flies. He fans his face with his bamboo hat. He hums some American rock 'n' roll song. He urges the buffalo into the jungle.

I cannot see my son anymore. I can only hear his voice growing more distant as it recedes into the background and my mother's voice swells louder again, carrying me away, faster and faster, over the red fields of opium poppies, their paper blossoms beckoning with promises and the sweet scent of oblivion.

"Given the apparent similarities between happiness and depression, it seems possible that endogenous happiness will be characterized by positive mood first thing in the morning, a heavy appetite, and persistent erotomania."

— Richard P. Bentall

Nadja Tesich

Mothers
A CHAPTER FROM
THE NOVEL **Native Land**

In the heat, the market carried the pungent odor of people and fruit. I bought cherries this time, ate them immediately, then remembered Rumanians and the cholera. I couldn't identify Rumanians but gypsies were everywhere this time, packs of kids with brilliant eyes and hair of different colors — black, blond, red. The guy selling *cilims* in the used objects section wasn't there, but in the same spot a woman sold spoons, silver, pots and pans. I bought a little lamp from her but didn't see anyone selling light bulbs. A man said, forget it, all gone. Don't bother with the roach spray either because it's imported from Croatia. He suggested his own remedies using baking soda, but he also said they were smart insects and do no harm, why kill them. Better than the rest of us sinners, we are the nastiest animal on earth, he said, sounding like somebody I knew.

In the café across the street, the waiter acknowledged me and in a gesture of friendliness lifted the tablecloth and shook the crumbs on the floor. "The same?" he said, remembering I liked my coffee medium bitter. The men remained the same — dark, gloomy, drinking the local brandy in small glasses while around us flies buzzed and the air was blue with smoke.

The paper continued to talk about national problems, bankruptcy, and transition. No mention of civil war. A whole page of pinups in string bikinis. More fashions. Hunger in the Soviet Union. Problems in the Ukraine. Racism in the US. Three pages of dead faces were still the most interesting, and I read each biography in detail. Some looked familiar. Several women looked like me. A dead actress made me think I should go see a play, at least one, before I go. In between the theater section and university lectures I saw a small article about AIDS. A hundred cases, they said, all imported. There was no mention of prevention, because it wouldn't work. Pharmacies were out of most things, the papers said, including heart medicine. I wondered if condoms had to be imported.

Light bulbs couldn't be found even in the largest hardware stores. A saleslady said maybe next week, but another one said it wasn't likely. The shortage had to do with the problems with Slovenia. "If they don't start sending us the bulbs we won't send them our meat, then let's see who wins," she said. The blond boy was from there, I remembered, the one I met at eighteen, and we made love in Dubrovnik on the beach.

All this left me with a lamp but no bulbs. You could get pissed. Without any premeditation I walked into the McDonald's restroom because it was the cleanest place to piss in and stole a light bulb. It was easy. I remembered Boris and the dog we stole once. We didn't intend to do it. The dog was there, following us. I should go see him, and see Mira too. Another time. Not yet. It would be talk, talk, explain, tell about her. Nothing can be explained, telling only makes it worse.

Walking away from McDonalds, I saw thousands of people in front of the Monument to the Revolution. They were shouting all sorts of things, with tons of new words. Many different parties, each with a slogan and a leader, different democrats, different radicals, but I didn't expect to see the bearded men behind the black flag; weren't they known as the killers when I was a kid, didn't thousands die for the red one?

Very confusing. Every possible flag was there except the old one. The killers and the enemies had changed, who were the good guys? Too bad Mama didn't live to see it all, but you never know, she might miss the old days. Without your enemies, how do you know you are you?

Don't get involved! Keep your mouth shut! It can be dangerous! At any moment somebody could point a finger and they'd find a reason to accuse me. What would be my guilt? Same as always, probably. Bad thoughts. Wrong position. Besides, what do I really know about their hatreds? No more than they know about mine. They must have a reason to be angry, why else would they be up in arms but I knew also that the other flag was part of my childhood, and I couldn't wipe it out even if I wanted to. I couldn't tell if my longing was for one or the other, I couldn't separate them, and then you can be nostalgic for things you didn't even like. Now that socialism was ending, did they expect you to snap and adjust overnight, let's forget everything, long live the new model. What hypocrites! They probably cheered until yesterday for the other side!

Will I be the last socialist? Nobody will dare admit it any more. I'll have to whisper about it behind closed doors, the way Mama whispered about monarchy.

A young man spoke on the podium, waving his arms, shouting against all sorts of people. The new anthem was familiar, they used to sing it in émigré circles in Chicago. The mob responded. And to what? Everything he said was muddled, without a single original word. And while he screamed, red in the face, against the past dictatorship, he was no different from those he wanted overthrown.

At least we had a theory, I thought, satisfied that there was a reason for my beliefs after all. Go give me a better theory than "each according to his need," and all the people I had admired believed in it too. There were Sartre, Yves Montand, both dead it's true.

Sometime during the new speech, I was aware that a short grandmotherly woman was watching me, like a cop, had even moved closer for another look. She wore a navy blue suit of that simple cut that had remained unchanged all over Europe for the last fifty years, with a matching bag, a chignon, and navy blue pumps. It was exactly what a middle class, middle-aged woman should look like, what all peasants aspired to; my mother had dressed that way. The woman's face seemed familiar but I didn't know from where. I watched her leave the man she was with, slowly she came towards me. I didn't move.

Her hand was on my shoulder. "Anna," she said with that painful stress on 'n', "it's you, isn't it?"

"A-n-n-n-a," it echoed on the street. Was that me? My old name, visible on the street, now struck me as thicker, wilder, more tragic than Ann, who was simple, reserved, and slender. Those two would not like each other, oh no. Good thing my body took no sides. Alone, to myself, I was maybe some other person. "Go, run, escape," a voice in me said. Too late. Trapped. No. I could speak French, or I could say sorry, a mistake, I'm someone else, I'm not who you think, but a part of me wanted to be found out, recognized as this person, while the other portion begged to be spared. " Yes," I said, giving in, "yes, it's me." This woman was not going to harm me, take me prisoner, she hugged, she kissed, she cried. "I knew it, I just knew it was you," she repeated, wiping her tears daintily, at the corners before they had a chance to spill over.

I knew her now because she wiped her tears with a silk handkerchief that was too small. She was a daughter of my mother's best friend, a feisty woman full of stories about her suitors and ghosts who came to visit at night. In her sentimental state, she changed entirely, became ladylike, maybe because of those embroidered silk handkerchiefs she used to wipe her eye with, so very delicately, the way you just don't see any more. And Zina, the daughter, was doing the same.

"Mishko," she shouted toward a man. "Why are you standing there like a pole, come here, look it's Anna, look, she hasn't changed at all."

"My husband," she said, introducing a tall man in his fifties in a suit and tie. "We've met already," he said, "maybe twenty years ago, at my mother-in-law's."

"Sure," I said, remembering only his profession, doctor — considered a very good match, the very best, what mothers aspired to, including my own.

"Mishko, I knew it was her, I just knew it, but I kept thinking, Zina, woman, your brain is gone, what would Anna do here in our misery."

"I didn't know you lived here," I said, not knowing what to say.

"Now we do. We moved four years ago because of the kids. Student dorms are horrible. How is your family?"

"Fine, everybody is fine," I said, hoping she won't ask for details.

"Zina, this will go on forever," he said, looking at the rally. "It gets worse."

"We were just having a little stroll," Zina said, "and now let's go have lunch. You can't even think about saying no. We wouldn't permit it."

Don't even think about it! If you didn't run away, the best is to give in. We walked slowly, Zina's arm under mine.

Their building had a massive old door and a turn of the century style; they said it was a private residence before the revolution. Zina huffed and puffed and complained about the lack of an elevator.

"It's only three floors," I said.

"Your shoes are comfortable," Zina said. "I wish I could wear them."

"Why can't you?"

"Be serious. They would make fun of me. An old lady in tennis shoes, they would say." She couldn't be more than a couple of years older than me.

The living room was modern — nicely furnished, sofas, bound books, and a wall unit with cups and festive plates. "We had a much bigger place at home, right off the main street, next to that big hotel, and Mom came over every day…oh well…" Zina said wistfully.

"It's not bad now," he said, "we converted the veranda into a bedroom. They have their own bedroom now."

"The kids?" I said.

"Yes," she said, "before all of us slept in this room. It was a bit crowded."

"Now she studies in the kitchen, he in the bedroom and we are here," she pointed toward couches in shades of brown and gold.

Mishko came out of the kitchen with coffee, sweet preserves, water and brandy on a plate. "Here, to your health!" he said raising his glass.

"To your homecoming!" she said.

"To us," I said.

They had taken their shoes off, how peaceful, how sweet they looked in their matching slippers, what was that smell coming from the kitchen, nutmeg? "How long are you staying?" he asked.

"Just passing through," I invented on the spot. "There was a conference on the coast so…"

"When was this?"

"A couple days ago."

"I wondered. Nobody is going there now. Did you see the papers? Most tourists have canceled. What a waste, oh my God…," Zina moaned. "Millions gone."

"Listen," I said, "don't tell Yanna if you see her. There is no way I can go…I'm leaving right away." I expected them to be shocked. Blood is blood, they would say. People travel days to visit the graves, and here she is without any excuse. Guilty. I was. For all sorts of things. Yanna was my mother's sister, Yanna was my only aunt.

"I understand," Zina said. "It would be tricky. The trains are on strike."

"Since when?"

"Two…three days ago."

"We are disintegrating," he said, "have you noticed?"

"I have," I said. "Tell me, what is happening, I am lost really. I understand the 'end of socialism,' but I didn't know we hated each other so much."

"Do we have to start on this?" Zina yelled. "That's all we talk about. You could go crazy."

"But I don't know," I said.

"I don't want to bore you with details," he said. "You were a kid when you left. You wouldn't understand much. But look at it this way — we've lost ourselves. Completely. Like a sick person. Worse than a physical illness. Massive schizophrenia. We don't know any longer who we are."

"Did we ever?"

"I don't know. I used to think we did but I'm no longer sure. I used to think our problem was that we never grew up. We never had time for it, or the right conditions. It was either the Communist slogans, or Western ones. Both deadly. Did you know that Africans from the remote areas when they come to Europe get TB immediately. Not immunized."

"Please, Mishko, don't start now on disease before lunch."

"I am trying to simplify our condition for someone from the outside, to reduce it to the basics."

"I don't care what you say," Zina said, lowering her voice as if somebody might be listening, the way her mother did always when talking about *them*, the Bolshevik vipers — "but our best times happened while *he* was alive. We lived well, we traveled, everything was quiet, no strikes, nobody heard of drugs, kids were polite. And now we might have a civil war, heaven forbid!"

"Sure," he said. "The corruption was covered up. Before only a few stole, now everybody does. Democracy…"

"We are not ripe for it," Zina said.

"Maybe not, but democracy implies some disorder."

"I don't like the disorder," Zina said. "I can't imagine anyone liking it." What's a light bulb, I thought about my own corruption, and besides I wasn't going to make a profit, just read a paper at night. "Where do you buy your light bulbs?" I heard myself ask.

"We stockpiled months ago," he said. "Do you need one, what's the problem?"

"They are out of them in the hotel," I said.

"Why don't you come here," Zina said. "Why be alone. You can have this couch. Promise you will…"

"I'm not staying, Zina, or I would…thanks anyway…."

"I wonder what's keeping them," Zina said, worried. "I can't complain, they are such good students, every exam on time. Maya is in a new field, ecology of rivers, and would like to go to California for a year but her boyfriend said no."

She stopped as if reminded of something more urgent. "Mishko," she said, "we're out of wine. Go get us a few bottles at the drugstore?"

When he closed the door, she picked up where she left off, "so, California for a year, that's what she wants. However, her boyfriend won't hear about it!"

"Tough!" I said, a bit too harshly.

"It's her boyfriend," Zina said with wide-open eyes. It meant, this is serious, this is her husband, her life, her future. "And…your husband…he lets you…alone?" she added.

"I don't ask him," I said, again with unnecessary harshness. I couldn't stand that question, "let's you…"

"You couldn't do it here," Zina said, "although the young are different, have you noticed, now you even see men with strollers, funny, ah? You know I retired early…last year. He was able to get a new job but I couldn't and it was strenuous. I spent three years on that train every weekend rushing here to cook."

"Zina! Are you serious? They would have managed. Three grown people."

"Sure, but they would have eaten junk, probably just opened cans and heated them up. It's unhealthy…. So, I retired and we came here but Mom took it hard. He really doesn't mind, your husband? You…don't get bored all alone?"

"No," I said. "I need to roam, I think. It's in my nature."

"Roam!" she laughed. "That's what you say now. If you had stayed here you wouldn't…it's because your mother decided to leave…that's why you are the way you are and why you look so young in those sneakers." She sounded jealous, or maybe not jealous but sad.

"I don't look young, Zina, go take a closer look! My hair is quite gray, see."

"It doesn't show. It blends in with the blond. And you move like a young girl."

"I danced ages ago," I said. Did she mean that everything I am right now is my mother's doing? That my mother is responsible entirely for my own dilemma, my doubts, and the way I walked? There was so much conviction in Zina's voice that I, Anna, would now be round, settled, and without my sneakers, in a wool suit and pumps. Even though I distinctly remembered I had come to the same conclusion a few days ago, now I opposed this woman in the same way I had opposed everything always, my America and their socialism. Out of pure stubbornness. My socialism was not like hers.

"Maybe not," I said, and a bit of my childhood came back, a portion so distant it appeared invented. "I ran away with the gypsies at five. They were horrified when they found me in the wagon, can you imagine, with all those stories about them stealing kids and all. They were very nice but I was disappointed when they took me back.

"I can't believe it!" Zina said. "You of all people! You looked so quiet, so perfect, even my mother said so."

"Quiet," I said. "Is that what I was?"

"Absolutely, quiet and dreamy, serious, a good student."

Like a spy, I thought, I wasn't quiet. I had bad thoughts. For movies and cherries I stole a dog, then sold it. And I led our gang against the butchers' boys. And here is this stolen light bulb. No, it's no. My dreams were bigger but they weren't girls' dreams. I wouldn't have been like her. No matter what they studied or did, it all ended up with cooking and kids. Just mothers and mothers and an occasional slut.

Here, I registered my own contradiction — what I intellectually disapproved of, bodily I had wished. They didn't mix.

"We ran into one of your friends the other day, the one who looked like that Mexican actress, dark with a small waist."

"Mira!"

"Her. She still looks adorable, still well dressed, you know how she was." Mira was adorable even in the first grade, how much I wished I could see Mira, we played hopscotch together.

Zena shuffled into the kitchen to check on something. I could smell parsley, carrots, everything cooking slowly, steaming the window panes.

"I'm so happy you are here, you can't imagine," she said. "My mama still mentions you in her prayers, you know she often goes to your grandma's grave. You helped us so much, did you know that? I wore nothing but the dresses you sent, I was the best dressed girl in school. I was even married in that dress, a beautiful white one with a high collar, tight bodice and a ballerina skirt. I wish I had kept that one but we sold it at some point."

I didn't know her well. She was just a serious girl a couple of years older than me, not the kind who roamed around the creek with boys. Her mother was more interesting, or maybe her stories were, how young, how pretty she was, how much she loved to dance, how tons of handsome men courted her and there was nothing left of it all.

"You must have some pictures?" I said, and Zina laughed, pleased, "You're still the same after all. Every time you came over, every single time you were in our house, you asked for the album. I could never figure out what you saw in it."

"Who knows," I said, not able to explain what I looked for. A clue of sorts. To everything.

From the wall unit, Zina produced two albums, leather bound and perfect, every picture in its place chronologically, nothing like my own two shoe boxes in New York, everything pell mell, people and the years.

Zina sat next to me, eager to tell, and began from the beginning. These albums were a story of her life, of the bright girl from my hometown who studied and then married well. The same photographer took the earlier pictures, in black and white; in the background, the same painted waterfall gave an illusion of depth. Did he kiss her foot too? Probably not. He gave me oranges, figs, an orange for a kiss. Then time passes and here is Zina in Belgrade, the street empty of cars. She is with Mishko, looking very shy, soon after her graduation. She'll get married in a month.

"God, you married so young," I said.

"No, not that young, Mama married at seventeen. Everybody married soon after college. Here! Do you remember?"

My graduation dress. I had worn it, that dress, just once. It must have looked spectacular here, even though it was made out of some artificial material, nylon or polyester, too hot for the summers in Chicago. The memory of loneliness inside that dress is bigger than that word, even now my throat tightens, I might stop breathing. The next moment, when the music stops, is erased. But I never danced like that again — it had become forbidden.

"We had a picture of you in it," Zina says, "at your mother's house, before the prom, but somebody stole it. You were so glamorous at that time, a real movie star. You're lucky, you've lived," she adds with some regret of her own.

"You looked much better than me in that dress," I say and mean it. It's nice that the same dress could stretch and serve for a happy wedding picture, what I see now.

Zina's life continued in the pictures chronologically — nothing had to be invented — her first job, which was her only job, and the husband was the only real boyfriend too. The first kid, a chubby, naked boy at the beach. On the island of Brac, she looks rounder. Another child, and a furniture set, still looking brand-new. This life was predictable and boring, but who can tell if change itself is an improvement except you get addicted to it like crack. I was starting to lecture again to someone, my sons, Marc, the whole world, wishing it weren't so.

"Are those your real teeth?" Zina's voice brought me back to earth.

"Why yes," I said, startled.

"I lost quite a few with kids…and you forget until it's too late. You always had beautiful teeth."

"Dad had good teeth," I said, a liar and a hypocrite. I took care of mine.

"Tell me," she said, "how do you manage to look so young? Is it America or what?"

"It's an illusion. I don't think I look young in New York. My guess is you don't know how to look at me."

Something was bothering her, poor Zina. Retired, with grown kids, maybe she had no real function, neither a young woman nor a grandmother. No hobbies either, nothing just hers.

"Do you still paint?" I asked. "Your pictures were all over the school."

"Oh you remember!" she said. "I stopped all that after high school. Who has the time?"

"You have all the time now," I said. "Hell, go and paint."

"What for?" Zina said, her eyes strangely Oriental. "It's too late now."

"For yourself!" I said, sounding like a cheerleader. At this instant, a full century separated us in practice, but there were other centuries we shared, some Ottoman misery in the soul.

"I'm sorry," Zina said, "I forgot to ask you…" No doubt, she was going to ask about my mother when the kids appeared at the door and I didn't have to circumvent the question because Zina had other things on her mind. "Please don't tell them it's all wonderful. They are stealing our kids," she whispered. Who is *they*?

"Guess where I found them?" Mishko said, beaming.

"At the drugstore," Zina said. "Are you hungry?"

The kids towered over me, am I shrinking or are they getting taller? Otherwise they were dark like him, and had her blue eyes, both dressed in blue jeans like my sons. And just like them, they wanted to eat right away. Zina looked at me nodding, see, do you understand why I had to come all that way on weekends to cook, see — my little angels, my darlings, my life, that's what you called your children.

She must have had it all prepared early in the morning, how else. The chicken soup came first, the very best, fragrant, full of carrots, greens, livers and so on, and the chicken was from a village because Zina was suspicious of the ones in the store. The sautéed breasts in lemon sauce came next, with potatoes au gratin and mixed salad which had her own dressing with dill, plus accidentally she had prepared *Blanche Neige*, the kids' and my favorite dessert, with floating egg whites in a thick sweet sauce. Nobody said anything serious. We ate nonstop.

"It's not an accident," the daughter said laughing. "We have something new every day, a cake, a rice pudding, a pie. She is the reason I can't lose weight. Would I be…"

"Don't look at Anna," Zina said. "You don't live in America. Here, men don't like bones."

"They are not that thin in America," I said.

"They certainly look that way," Zina said.

"Just movies," I said.

It was such a good lunch after which you lie down for an hour or so, stomach full, mind empty, but damn it, even here America kept interfering. Question and answer period!

"You see," the boy started, like an elder in the village tradition, "first she wants to go for a year to California. What if everybody left?"

"I only want to go for a year," the girl said, "who is talking about immigration?"

"That's what you say now," Zina said, "what if you meet…"

"I'm curious," the boy said, "they are obsessed only with money, aren't they? I mean it comes up in all the films. It's true, isn't it?"

"Yes," I said. "You're right." How much do you make, how much is he worth, a million dollars, thanks a million, looks like a million, time is money, bankable, get a star. "Yes, it can't be denied," I explained. "I would say money is to them what food is to us."

"Well said," said the husband. "Well observed."

"But food is different…there is a memory of hunger here while money is abstract."

"I agree with you," I said. "Money is not a childhood wish."

"What is the wish?" the girl said.

"I don't know," I said, "what was in the beginning. Love maybe."

"We talk about money too," Zina said, "and how!"

"Mama, it's different," he said, "sure we do…how much is bread and meat today and so on. The idea of making money and wanting more all the time even when you have enough is foreign to us. It would have to become symbolic first."

"What do you study?" I said.

"Economics," the boy laughed, "don't I sound like it?"

"No, you don't."

"Mama told us you are in the theater."

"Sort of."

"Everybody thought you'd go into medicine. You were such a good student," Zina said. "Theater is so…unpredictable." Zina meant risqué, almost like being with the circus.

"Personally," the girl said as if to herself, "I think they are obsessed with sex."

"Who is obsessed?" Zina said, surprised.

"Americans, in films," her daughter explained looking at me. "Why do they talk about it so much, why don't they just do it, I mean why make a whole film about sex."

"I don't know," I said, "maybe sex is to them what nationalism is here. It used to be forbidden. America is a puritan country…it's hard to explain, we don't have it here, do we, sex as evil and temptation. Look, money and sex you can get if you try, while love is harder, maybe sex is a substitute too, a second choice to the original wish…but I am no expert…just rambling."

"I've heard," the girl said, "they make love on the phone and they never see a person. A friend of mine says, that's what they do in New York…."

"I've heard," the boy said, "that they send sex messages on computers and that it's even worse. You never even hear a person."

"We are exhausting her," the father said.

"Let's say I went for a year," the girl said stubbornly.

"Could she have a job before she got there?" the mother asked.

"I doubt it. It would take a while, people look for jobs all the time, lose them, get new ones, especially now."

"All the time," Zina gasped.

"Not all the time. Often."

"Apartments too?" Zina asked

"Yes."

"Why?"

"For different reasons, money, jobs, change. They love to change over there. They really do."

"It takes a lot of energy, all that," Zina said. "I wouldn't like it."

"It's not for everyone," I said.

"But if I get a scholarship…" the girl started.

"Who is it for?" the boy said.

"Young people, strong. It's better for plumbers than poets, that's for sure. I'm serious."

"See what I mean," Zina said. "Do you remember a classmate of mine, Ivan? He flunked out of school, a real troublemaker, well, he now has a fancy restaurant in LA. Came back last year with a big car. It's a strange country," Zina added.

Ivan? The butcher's son? I agreed inwardly that this type of person had a better chance in the US than Boris who had studied philosophy, but Zina was making Ivan too attractive with his car and no degree, and was defeating her very purpose in what was meant to be bad publicity. Instead of repulsion, the USA shone, madly fascinating, if someone like Ivan could do so well.

"It's best to see for yourself," I said. "Why couldn't she go for a year?" My attempt at subversion.

"What if everybody left," the boy said. They didn't want her to go.

"What if she fell in love," Zina said. She wasn't going.

"She'll go for a year, and she'll come back," I said.

"Could you live here?" Zina switched the subject, sneakily. "We always thought you'd come back some day. Everyone did. Kids, Anna left a real-life drama behind her, this poor man, my classmate, was madly in love, poor David and he never got over it, took to drinking, wasted his life. They say his mother died from pure grief."

"Please," I said. "How could I ever do so much?"

"Mama, you ask a question, then you drop it, she didn't even have a chance to answer it," the daughter said, turning toward Anna. "She does it all the time."

"What was the question?" Zina said.

"Could she live here. What would you miss about America?"

"I don't know, I haven't thought about it," I said. "Here people look at you too much, in New York you can be invisible.... What would I miss…maybe an illusion of freedom, not political but the other one."

Soon I found myself talking as if the CIA had paid me, about a mythical America, the open roads that extend forever across the immense land and if you fail in Chicago you pick up elsewhere, St. Louis, Phoenix, L.A. and you just keep going, stopping occasionally to refuel. Infinite possibilities, you can invent yourself, and become someone else, the country is so big, no end to it. It was a song to America from one of my plays. A tribute to the dream. The dream was good. The best dream ever.

From this angle, with them, well fed, warm, I loved this country I had created on paper and the mythical search from New York to L.A. had its own heroic scale while the old and new selves circled around the traveling person as angels without disturbing.

Coming to the end, I felt disturbed, schizophrenic, didn't I condemn all that just recently. Yes. Didn't I strive for unity? On the other hand, why can't a human being contain more then one governing idea, why not two or three? Didn't Marc say that the real proof of superior intelligence is the capacity to hold two opposite views and not fall apart?

"So much, work, all that, moving searching," Zina said. "Do you know anyone who lives normally?"

"The way I see it," father said, "if we didn't have America, we would have some other country. America just happened first. My fear is that young people can't see well because they are only attracted to the surface of things. Communism harmed us, especially our middle class, but it never destroyed the family. Capitalism will. Now we have whole villages without men, all gone to Germany, when they come back they bring the worst with them. Topless bars and striptease. Drugs. I see America only as the largest symptom and no more."

I saw it in my own way — if everyone, kids, husband, and wife were running off, each in the name of self-realization — this lunch I had loved wouldn't exist or it would be a different lunch, or it might happen once in six months but then it wouldn't be the same. Like making love once in six months. A big to-do, so to speak. I shifted my position again — was aware of it — a moment ago, I had felt bad for Zina, who had nothing to look forward to now that the kids are grown up, a woman who could have done things. Wrong again. Zina's life was not wasted — this was a happy family, all in all, bright kids, nice husband, why would she be better off if daily she appeared with her briefcase around seven, and then spoke about her job and her company nonstop? Who is getting exploited, I ask you? They slept in one room and most likely didn't fight about each other's space. The kids won't have major gripes against the parents, accuse them of indifference. The parents gave everything and children will give everything back in turn, that's how it was. But it will all change, very soon, any moment now — women like Zina will be gone — no more grandmas left, just women searching for "new maturity" in their special units, searching for the better retirement spots. In towns designed for them away from teenagers and noise. And then young couples will have their own segregated quarters too.

Happiness, I concluded my silent lecture, was not about the unlimited opportunities and roads that go forever. Maybe it's about something limiting, attainable, as small as this apartment, this lunch, the nap we took next, Zina and I on her couch.

Outside, on the street, the air carried the strong scent of linden trees, mixed with cooking smells here and there; somewhere in the distance I heard the church bells. At that moment in the orange light just before the darkness, the city appeared like a beautiful man, a gypsy with shiny eyes. A short-lived magic hour, then very fast everything will vanish with a red blood sun.

I had done nothing but eat and sleep the whole day, yet now my body was wide-awake; light in my sneakers, I wanted to go dancing. At the same time, my head whirled with images flying in all directions, Zina, her album, her food, my dresses, the puzzle, the mystery of everything. Zina, my mother's friend's daughter, is what Mama had wished for me, except the poor woman never got that satisfaction. That's what "middle class" meant, that type of order. Good kids, good food, everyone together. There was nothing about them I objected to, on the contrary, but now, on the street, alone once again, I knew that was not me, never could be. From the outside, I had all the trappings — schools, job, and my comfortable apartment mother had approved of, but Zina was inside it all, she believed it, while at best I could pass, if I tried hard. A part of me always escaped, didn't want to be caught by order.

Not bad, my answers about America. Nothing to be ashamed of. It was one thing to hate privately for personal reasons and your own satisfaction but I had always been a fair person and a fair teacher, had refused to simplify anything for anyone, either this country or the US. It's a part of me I approved of, the constant part of my person, the one that's most like Marc, some intellectual stubbornness in both of us, not to give in to stupidity. No, America can't be described in a word or two. Not a nation. A continent. After all those years, still a mirage. It's good I didn't tell the worst about it, I could have. Was I trying to protect it for the outsiders, the same way some women do when they say "Oh my husband has his good side." Or was I protecting my sons, Marc, and me?

The street I walked on was deserted. The orange glow had faded, soon the night will fall. The church bells continued, a dark sound, thick. Did they ring this way before Belgrade was bombed? My mind kept jumping from this to that, from Zina to *Blanche Neige*, to her mother and mine and nothing was simple, not even that word mother. When I said *mother, mom*, in English, I saw a particular person, nobody I had known, maybe an ad on TV, who the hell knows — but *mom*, American mom, is a woman in Bermuda shorts fixing sandwiches, calmly and efficiently placing bandaids on, soon she will drive a whole bunch of kids to a baseball game. It's not as if she didn't feel bad occasionally, sure she did, and often she wasn't sure she was doing enough, and then she read books on child care. I had never known a woman like this yet I suspect this mom really exists, the way the French *maman* does some where in Paris or Lyon, always charming, always flirtatious, laughing and kissing while putting the kids to bed. None of these mothers change, their pictures remain constant year after year and the native one is always the same too — *majka* who cooks constantly and whose face is sad beyond words. She is the opposite of the other two — heavy, like bread, like earth, like graves, she often wears black because somebody is always dying and she is always feeding sons who'll go off to war and then she'll have to bury them too.

But there is only one mother, you can't shop for her, pick and choose, reject, think about if maybe she is just right for you. Just one, I thought on the street as the light faded completely. No other would ever be as good, and this one loved too much, excessively, you could never shake her off. The biggest love ever. No other country would ever be as good. It's not the fault of the US. Of course not. It simply paled in comparison. This type of love isn't good for the economy, it creates attachments to people, places, graves, no wonder they have a different type of mother over there, a cooler sort who traveled in wagons, away from friends, was lost over and over again, suffered and loved alone. And the search for happiness is good for the economy too, imagine if everybody were contented with a minimum, let's say two summer dresses, just imagine, no, capitalism couldn't exist without the lack of something, wanting to get it, the search for substitutes, all those needs dying to get fulfilled and yet never knowing. Never knowing propelled everything, and you never knew if the real thing or the substitute propelled you, the new need created while you were running to fulfill the first, a mutation of the need. I couldn't figure out if the nervousness came first and then the economy, or if the economy created everything, or if perhaps they were so intertwined you couldn't separate them. Obsessively going, unable to stop, my head kept asking impossible questions while my feet stumbled in the dark.

There was nobody in the lobby. Silence. The manager was gone. He has not been there for awhile, was he replaced? No other sounds anywhere, nobody watched TV. Maybe I was all alone in the hotel at night.

The lamp and the light bulb didn't work, maybe there was something wrong with the socket or the cord. There was no music downstairs on a Sunday night and I welcomed the cries from the room across the hall; either the same couple or some other went on killing each other and I felt less alone. I wished I had told Zina about her, why not? Maybe next time. I can talk about her now, I won't fall apart or anything. I can even say aloud, she is dead, my mother is dead. It's over.

Mark Anthony Jarman

Hoarse Latitudes

Times one thinks: Is this my fuzzy penance? Is this what they warned us of all those withering Sundays at the Cathedral? Things have goofed up on me. I drive and I pull in from the Interstate into hamburger midnights, main streets of Montana watching out for the black & whites, the ghosts, the radar and antennae and satellites over the land of the free and the dead, the shifting eyes and crewcuts and legs sweating on the seats of genuine Corinthian leather. We head down to the big Helix Hotel, catch the latest reincarnation of say Hank Snow or Elmore James on an overdriven Hamer lead guitar, a bottleneck slide, open D tuning, hoppy New Zealand beer on special. Soon come we're sloppy drunk at the blues club, scarfing chicken wings and carrots and angels on horseback.

"He has a different sound, you know what I'm saying? Doesn't squeeze the high E all the time." They're doing a thrash version of "Born Under A Bad Sign": "Bad luck and trouble, my only friend...." At this exact point his tube amp explodes, the back melting, giving off firecracker sounds. This makes me think: some people trust only in tragedy. I wonder if this is not true of me, some latent Celtic ghost of me addicted to things falling apart, blues going out of tune, polychrome smoke, and explosions.

To change your spots, to make the past obey, lie down like a pet, a favored spaniel: this should be easy; pruning the tragedies-in-the-making, to settle for luck.

Yes, board that bus or golden train away from your childhood bungalow or your first young wife and you think, Now I'm done with all this, and are right but not in any way you know. Eventually you'll crawl an ugly carpet wishing that shining train never left the station, wishing to dip your burning face once more in the clear childhood river, to ride your bike to the Public Beach concession for a bottle of Creme Soda, bats veering around the one purple street lamp to negotiate with the insects of night. After the lovely Mexican woman has hung up on you, pound the basement floor with your fists, try to really hurt that ugly carpet. I had a crush on my Grade 6 teacher; her wedding that year did not change this one iota, it seemed off in another land. The song "To Sir With Love" brought tears to my eyes: it was about her. With some fury we chased her bridal car outside the church, and she laughed and blushed in the window. I don't remember a husband even being there. She married me, took my Grade 6 body in. In Grade 7 the radio sang "kiss him and hug him and kiss him" all summer long, and I hoped Mary Jane in Jasper was listening. I saw her in September and necked down the ravine. She *was* listening. Was it a girl group? Phil Spector? Leslie Gore? I can't remember but now there is a few thou of body damage and insurance won't cough up, insurance won't cover the nut. As a kid I picked hazelnuts and wild blueberries, saskatoons, and strawberries with real cream from the hillbilly farm on the curve of the road, then the first cigarette, the last clean breath of youth. We built huge cigarettes from hollow reeds and desiccated poplar leaves. The family dentist said what in tarnation is this black stuff on your teeth? You're out fumbling in the middle of the mandatory minor evils and the parents would need night goggles; they can't see. You have no real form to them yet. Their sense of time passing is utterly different, stalled. The idea of you in diapers is too vivid still, it's hard to reconcile that with you into that schoolgirl's foreign bra straps, her mysterious new neck. They find the pearl earring and the frost-white lip gloss outside your window. Mouths everywhere. Androgynous airports. Footsteps. I still want to neck down the ravine, but the ravine has receded. I attempt to be nicer to my parents, to write old friends, to be kinder to my Intended. The ravine evades me.

Mid-Columbia River Indians: (l–r) Cynthia Espirito and Melinda Kishwalk, White Salmon, Washington. Photo by Jacqueline Moreau.

Mid-Columbia River Indians: The Spino family, Lyle, Washington. Photo by Jacqueline Moreau.

"…once the debilitating consequences of happiness become widely recognized it is likely that psychiatrists will begin to devise treatments for the condition and we can expect the emergence of happiness clinics and anti-happiness medications in the not too distant future."

— Richard P. Bentall

Craig Lesley

Train Time

CHAPTER ONE FROM THE
NOVEL **The Sky Fisherman**

My stepfather Riley Walker worked for the Union Pacific Railroad, and it was a steady job, but uncertain, because trucking had hurt the railroad by then and they were cutting back. Riley had only a little seniority, and he was always getting "bumped," a railroad term that meant moving to another job when you were forced out by someone with more seniority who wanted yours. In turn, my stepfather bumped someone with less seniority than he had. As a result, my childhood was spent moving from one railroad town to another, each one smaller and more remote than the one before. This constant moving gave me a sense of restlessness, of always being near the edge of something, but of freedom, too, and loss. I learned that I didn't have to feel attached to anyone, except my mother, stepfather, and my Uncle Jake, and even that changed eventually.

My mother faced these frequent moves with patience and relentless good cheer for the most part. Her first item of business was to measure the new windows. Then she sewed bright, colorful curtains and seemed even cheerier once they were hung. "That civilizes the place a bit," she'd say, and Riley would nod and agree, "Just like home."

I'd glance up from the railroad housing linoleum — it was my task to scrub the floors with disinfectant, trying to remove any trace of germs left by the former tenants — and I'd try to say something encouraging. But the packing and loading were always difficult, and we worked like coolies, if you want to know the truth.

The moving pattern was recognizable. After we'd been in a place about a year, one night Riley would delay coming home while he stopped off for a couple hours at a tavern near the railroad depot commiserating with the buddies he'd be leaving, and working up his nerve enough to tell my mother. Supper finished, she'd stand anxiously by the door, sipping a cup of hot tea and watching the twilight settle. Riley always carried a small gift when he arrived late — candy or scented candles perhaps, and she'd thank him and reheat dinner, while I went in the front room to watch TV and sulk.

They'd talk with lowered voices at the kitchen table, and I'd hear the clink of Riley's fork and knife, my mother fixing more tea. Her voice always caught a few times, and one phrase I'd hear was, "Riley, when's all this going to stop?" Then he'd attempt to say soothing, comforting words such as he was building up seniority all the time, or he'd heard the schools were good in Harney or Grass Valley, small towns near the railroad sidings where we lived. When the towns became too small to offer comfort, he'd say it was good for a boy to have room to roam, and rural people still had good values.

After they went to bed, I usually didn't hear anything except a few sighs, until the night my stepfather announced we were moving clear across the state to Griggs. Then my mother cried.

And in the morning hours, I went to the bathroom sink for a cold glass of water and found her lying naked on the tile floor. A wet washcloth covered her face, and her skin seemed flushed, as if she had a fever. My turning on the light had startled her, and she bolted upright for a moment, whipping the washcloth from her eyes and calling out, "Griggs! Griggs!" Then she settled back like a child in a restless sleep.

We'd usually have about two weeks before the actual move, enough time to make arrangements for the mail, utilities, and phone. I'd mope around school a little, wringing sympathy from my teachers and a few classmates. Most of the kids had lived on family farms, generation after generation, and I was just a newcomer to them anyway. The teacher might suggest a going-away gift, and the class would bring dollars to buy a book or a basketball. They'd dutifully sign their names and I'd promise to remember them and write, but of course I never did.

My mother always conferred with my teachers and took careful notes about my subjects, so I wouldn't fall behind in the shuffle. She dressed well for those conferences, and when I saw her standing alongside my teachers, I was surprised how pretty she was and how her ash-blond hair shone in the sunlight. "Pretty enough for Hollywood," Riley always teased, but my mother claimed it wasn't true, on account of her nose, which was a little sharp.

Riley tried to ease the strain of displacement by buying some things my mother treasured. A love seat with matching needlepoint chair and a drum table with a leather top come to mind. These nice pieces of furniture were always purchased on time, and I remember how odd they looked in the small plain houses where we lived.

My Uncle Jake usually helped with the moves. He was my father's brother and had been fishing with him when my father drowned in a boating accident on the Lost River. After that, Jake tried to keep an eye on us, but he was a bachelor by nature, and I always thought he was relieved when my mother remarried. I knew my mother blamed Jake and his recklessness for my father's death — but she never said much. The Griggs move was our seventh, and my mother didn't call Jake to tell him about it because she knew he was so involved with his sporting goods store and guide business that he couldn't spare the time.

My mother always tried to appear happy while packing, and occasionally, she whistled. Before each move, she made a triple batch of her three bean salad, because you could eat it hot or cold, and her Oriental Sesame chicken for the same reason. Sometimes, the power wasn't turned on at the new place, and it took a while to settle.

For the Griggs move Riley hired two casual laborers from the hall in town, and that pair hardly moved at all. One had highwater pants that barely grazed the top of his runover boots, and the second owned a stomach as big as a flour sack, so he had to sit down frequently to wait out his "woozy" spells. Each man heaped several helpings of chicken and salad on his plate, and the first said the chicken reminded him of being in the Philippines during his tramp schooner days. The other kept pushing the food around his plate with a piece of white bread. "Mighty good fixings," he said. When they were out of earshot and gouging the drum table while loading the truck, my mother glared at Riley and muttered, "I guess we've still got a ways to slip."

Moving to Griggs was a slide. We lived in railroad housing at the siding itself. The reality was I'd have to take the school bus thirty-five miles to Pratt for my junior year. My mother would have to do without the comforts of a nearby town. "I'll just catch up on my reading," she said when she realized the situation.

As always, we started out hopeful but as we traveled across miles and miles of desolate country, a pall fell over our little band. Riley gripped the U-Haul truck's steering wheel as if trying to seize control of his life. I sat staring out the window at sagebrush and sparse juniper trees, a few jack rabbits, and an occasional loping coyote. "Good hunting around here I'll bet," Riley said when we saw a covey of chukars eating gravel at the roadside.

Griggs was one of those remote railroad sidings with three buildings and a lot of dust. All painted leprous yellow, the buildings varied in size with the largest for the stationmaster and the smallest for the trackwalker. Ours was the middle house and sported a strip of cheatgrass-infested lawn. In the early June heat, the buildings appeared to undulate, and my mother said, "Riley, we're going to need some fans."

Beyond the railroad tracks was a sluggish, dirty brown river with a fringe of willows. Close to the river, the air seemed rank and stagnant, offering little relief from the heat. The one outstanding item I noticed at Griggs was a decent basketball hoop and backboard fastened to one of the telegraph posts just beyond the trackwalker's shack. The hoop had a new nylon net. I had been the sixth man for the Grass Valley team the past year and figured I could have started my junior year, especially with two senior guards going off to college. But Pratt was smaller and I knew I could play B-league ball with no trouble at all, maybe even move to forward, so I planned to keep my shooting touch sharp over the summer.

That basket was the only thing I felt good about. Still, we started fixing our house with a vengeance — hanging curtain rods and curtains, lining the shelves with contact paper, covering the pitted Formica table with a bright blue tablecloth.

My mother's face had dropped when she saw the bathroom though, which had only a shower unit. She was accustomed to long baths soaking away her worries and doubts. When she pointed out this lack of a tub to Riley, he just spread his hands wide. "It's only temporary, Flora," he said. "I'm building seniority all the time."

Dwight Riggins, the Griggs' station agent, was a burly man with black hair the color of creosote. He kept four or five cigars tucked into the bib pocket of his striped coveralls. The day we arrived in Griggs he was away, but he showed up later that evening just in time to help us unload some heavy items like the refrigerator from the front of the truck bed. My mother had put lamp shades in the refrigerator to keep them from getting crushed and Dwight thought that was a pretty nifty trick. "After you move a few times, you learn some little shortcuts," she told him.

"I'm sure you do at that," he said. He seemed friendly enough and I was glad for his help, because by that time we were all getting pretty tired. Still, I didn't care for the way he kept sneaking sidelong glances at my mother, and I thought maybe his laugh came just a little too easy. It turned out that he was batching a couple weeks because he had dropped off his wife and daughter at a fancy art camp.

"They're taking painting classes at the coast," he explained. "Both of them together. It's a mother-daughter deal."

"It must be cool at the coast," my mother said, and I could hear the touch of envy in her voice. "I'll bet it's quite lovely."

"It better be, for what I'm paying for that program," he said. "My wife doesn't have a lick of talent, but Dwy-anne, my daughter, there's another story. Of course the teacher tells them both they're gifted. That's how he affords living on the coast in summer."

After Dwight left to have dinner in town with some friends, my mother strolled through the house checking the layout. Even though the boxes hadn't been unpacked, the beds were made and the furniture set out — so you had a sense of the place. She ran her fingers over the dusty doorsill and looked out over the dry countryside. "We're going to need some fans, Riley, if this is going to be tolerable."

"I'll put them on my list, Flora," he said.

"There's more to Dwight than meets the eye," Riley told me later. At first I thought he was talking about Dwight's sidelong glances at my mother but then Riley said, "He's a nudist. Word has it the whole family is — even the daughter. And she's just a couple years older than you are."

I stopped unpacking one of my suitcases. He had piqued my interest. "How do you know that?" I asked.

"Railroad telegraph," he said. "Word gets around."

"He had clothes on today."

Riley shook his head. "He's not a nudist on railroad time. They'd dock him. But you'd better keep an eye on his daughter."

As section foreman, Riley's job was to drive the speeder car twenty miles either side of Griggs, checking for loose or rotten ties. After he found them, he ordered a section crew out from Pratt to replace the ties while he supervised their work. At times they had to delay the trains a few hours to complete repairs. Riley always carried his shotgun with him in the speeder, a Remington model 870 pump with a barrel cut down to exactly the legal eighteen inches. Over the years he'd brought home a lot of game with that shotgun, and I've got memories of Riley hunching over the outside faucets cleaning birds because my mother didn't want blood and feathers in her kitchen sink, although she enjoyed eating the birds out of the pan, if they were fried crisp.

During the first two weeks we were in Griggs, Riley had me ride with him in the speeder as far as Barlow, a siding almost identical to Griggs but twenty miles east. On the return trip, we saw a covey of chukars eating gravel on the railroad bed and Riley handed me the shotgun. "Sluice them, Culver," he said.

Usually I wait for birds to fly but chukars prefer to run and these started racing down the track. With the first shot, I stopped two and as the rest flew, I got one bird but missed completely with my third shot. At home Riley bragged a little about my dead-eye aim. He held up birds for my mother to inspect. "By god, they look like bandits don't they," he said, referring to the markings around their eyes.

"You know it's not the season, Riley," she said

As we were cleaning them out back, he spoke slowly, "Your mother's acting pretty quiet."

I had noticed but I said, "Maybe she's just tired."

"She's always adjusted before, but this place takes a little more getting used to."

I wanted to say something comforting but I couldn't think of anything.

"Well," he said. "It's only temporary. I'm building up seniority all the time." A BB fell out from underneath the skin of one of the chukars, plinking against the metal pan. "Watch your teeth, Culver. We can't afford any trips to the dentist."

Late that evening, when the fierce heat of the day slacked, a cool breeze came up from the river. In the twilight before dark, it seemed momentarily pleasant in Griggs. After returning from town, Dwight sat on his screened porch reading the paper. A match spurted, and after a while, we could smell his cigar in the evening air. My mother, Riley, and I walked out to a little knoll overlooking the river. Ducks rose from the shallows and winged overhead with that soft whistling ducks make as the wind catches their feathers.

"That water looks good enough for a swim," Riley said. "Anybody want to join me?"

"I don't feel that adventuresome," my mother said. "Anyway, my swimsuit is still packed somewhere."

"No one's going to see much way out here," Riley said, stripping down to his undershorts and wading in. "Hey, this feels great."

He was trying to have a good time so I joined him even though my heart wasn't in it. The water did feel good and I liked the way the mud squished under my toes.

Just after ten o'clock, the Coastal Flyer came by, its cars shining silver under the summer moon. We saw the people inside — first the coach cars and then the lounge car and diner. White-jacketed waiters hovered over the people eating dinner, and by looking close, I could glimpse the single red rose on each table. I envied the people on the train because they seemed to be going somewhere, and I could imagine how Griggs must have appeared to them in the moonlight — just a little, no-count railroad siding with the three of us looking like stick figures. And then Riley surprised me, surprised us all, by dropping his undershorts and grabbing his ankles, flashing those passing diners a full moon.

I heard my mother suck in her breath, then say, "Don't be so uncouth, Riley. Remember, you actually *work* for the railroad."

"I don't work for *them*," he said, meaning the diners.

"Well, of course, you're setting a poor example for the boy," she said. "In any case, Culver and I have ridden on the train and we have enjoyed a wonderful dinner. And I'm certainly glad my appetite wasn't spoiled by seeing some man's hind end."

Riley didn't answer but managed to wink at me as he pulled up his shorts.

My mother sighed and I knew she was thinking about the time we rode the train to see my Uncle Jake in the beautiful, mountainous part of the state. I was nine. She intended to talk with him about my father's death — "To clear the air," as she put it.

My mother had saved some money so we could eat in the dining car. Before dinner, I went into the men's lounge and slicked my hair back. She had brought along my Sunday school white shirt and an old tie that had belonged to my father. The tie was blue with a hand-painted leaping red fish. She had cut the tie and resewn it to fit, although it remained a little long.

The waiter provided us with menus and stubby pencils to mark our choices. The pencils had no erasers, so I was careful not to make a mistake. She ordered lamb chops with spearmint jelly, and when the chops came, each one had a little parsley ruffle around the blackened bone, and I didn't think I'd ever seen anything so elegant before. My mother had me taste the jelly, which came in a small white paper cup. "They make it from crushed mint leaves," she said. "It's nice when they go out of their way to make things special."

It was good, sweet and pungent at the same time, although I preferred my cheeseburger.

We sat at the window a long time, watching the countryside roll by. Once I saw a farmer changing headline in his alfalfa field. Glancing up from his work, he took off his red cap and waved it at the train. I waved back, even though I doubted he saw anything but the train sliding by sleek as wind.

"I could get used to this," my mother said, pouring herself another cup of tea. Out the window, scenery rushed by and the setting sun lengthened the shadows of tall pines. Farmhouse lights were beginning to wink on.

Now, standing by that remote siding, my mother stared at the Coastal Flyer's brake lights dimming in the distance.

"Better times are coming," I said because I couldn't think of anything else.

After a moment, she said, "I expect they're just around the corner."

The third Friday after we'd moved in, my stepfather was away on the speeder checking on the tie repairs the section crew was making near Barlow. Dwight watched me shooting baskets for a while from his front porch, then came off and challenged me to a game of one-on-one. I figured he'd be easy, because he looked slow and clumsy in his usual coveralls and clodhoppers. But today he was wearing tennis shoes, and when he stripped down to a t-shirt and shorts, I saw he was no pushover. He was remarkably quick for a man his size, and I could seldom drive on him, so I had to rely on my outside shot, which was always streaky. If Dwight had the ball, he backed in, using his bulk to keep me away, then put up soft hooks or twisting jump shots. Luckily, he was rusty and soon became winded, or I might have lost.

My mother brought a chair from inside the house and placed it on the yard, first turning on the lawn sprinkler to get a little cool moisture. She'd made sun tea by leaving a pitcher of tea bags and water in the sun, and she poured some of this over a tumbler of ice. She sat, sipping her tea and reading Hollywood gossip magazines.

After finishing the game, Dwight approached my mother's chair and tried to make conversation, but he was awkward at it. "This kid is a regular whiz," he said. "All he needs is to pack a few more pounds." He dribbled the ball a couple times and tried to palm it, but it slipped away. "I used to play college ball myself at a Mormon school in Utah. But I'm not Mormon."

"That explains the cigars then, doesn't it," my mother said. "We're not Mormon either."

"No, I didn't think you were," he said. "Not for a minute."

She offered him a glass of tea, but he declined and then unwrapped the cellophane from one of his cigars. "Cuban. I've got a friend who flies down there on business. He tells me these cigars are rolled on the damp thighs of young Cuban girls. Fidel sees to it they're all under sixteen. That's the rule."

I had never heard anyone make such a remark in front of my mother before, and I didn't know how she would react. She placed the glass of ice tea against her cheek and laughed softly. "I imagine that's why you enjoy them so much," she said. "You and your friend must have *extremely* active imaginations."

He seemed pleased that he had impressed her and turned to me. "What do you think, Sport? You want to try one of these dusky beauties? Let's see, those girls would be just about your age."

"I don't believe he'd care for one," my mother said. She held the glass of tea against her forehead. "Culver's interests lie in an entirely different direction, don't they Culver?" Before I could answer she added, "So perhaps you should hang on to the cigars you have."

"You got a point there all right," he said.

It seemed for a minute he was going back to his house, but then he spoke again. "When I see you sitting out in this heat just reading those magazines, it makes me wonder if there isn't something else you might do. Develop some interests."

She ran her finger around the sweaty beaded outside of the glass and touched it lightly to her lips. "I have interests," she said. "There's the boy." She tipped the glass slightly in my direction. "And I'm very interested in travel. Now you must excuse me. I've got to think about supper." With that she folded her magazine and headed into the house.

From Griggs, it was three miles to Griggs Junction, a combination restaurant and truck stop crested with a blue neon eagle whose flashing wings imitated flying. On paydays, Riley enjoyed taking us there for what he called a "fling," and as we drove in, he'd wave at all the truck drivers and call out, "How's it going, George." He had greeted strangers the same way ever since I had known him, and when I was younger, I had marveled that he knew so many men named George.

This night, my mother had put on a cool green dress that emphasized the green in her hazel eyes. As she looked out the window at the parking lot filled with trucks, she seemed restless. When she put on a pair of new sunglasses she must have bought in town, I swear she could have been a movie star, sharp nose or not.

Grinning, Riley looked at me as if to say, "How'd you think I ever got so lucky."

"Do you have any fresh fruit," my mother asked the waitress when she came to take the orders. "It's so hot today, I'm feeling like a fruit salad would be just the thing."

The waitress scowled at the question. "We had some bananas but the flies got them." She tapped her pen against the pad to get the ink going. "Sure has been hot. Earlier, they couldn't get the kitchen fans working, and it's like a boiler room back there. Honey, let's see now, we've got some canned peaches and cottage cheese. Or some pears."

"Pears and cottage cheese would be just fine," my mother said, and handed her the folded menu.

"I sure do like that dress," the waitress said. "It probably doesn't come in my size."

Riley and I had cheeseburgers as always, and I had a large chocolate shake. This was only late June and I figured July and August were going to be unbearable. I'd written a letter to my uncle Jake about trying to fix me up with a job in the sporting goods store, and I was wondering if it was air conditioned. I hadn't told Riley or my mother, but if the job came through, I knew she'd approve.

A golden curtain above the counter opened and a little puppet band played music along with the juke box. My mother tapped her fingers to the tunes.

"We should go dancing sometime," Riley said. "We haven't been dancing since that night in Black Diamond. Geez, that seems years ago."

"It was," my mother said. "Black Diamond was Culver's first year in junior high school — five moves back."

Riley winced a little. "I'm getting old fast."

My mother glanced in his direction, but she didn't say anything.

When the food came, Riley and I started eating ours, but my mother asked for a salad plate and then separated the pears from the cottage cheese. The cottage cheese did appear affected by the heat, and when she held a forkful to her nose, she wrinkled it. She cut the pears into very small bites and ate slowly. When she had finished and laid down her fork, Riley asked, "How was your salad, Flora?"

"It's a sorry business, Riley," she said. "A very sorry business altogether. Excuse me, I'm going to need the ladies' room."

After she was gone, Riley put another quarter in the jukebox so the puppet band played again. "She's in a mood," he said.

"It's been hot," I said and sucked on my milkshake.

He tried singing along with the music but he gave it up shortly. After what seemed a long time, he took the railroad watch from his pocket. "She must be having a session in there." A few more minutes passed. "She had one of those after we ate Chinese food that time in Grass Valley. You remember? She was gone over half an hour that time."

"I remember all right," I said. I was only eleven then and didn't remember too clearly.

He put a couple quarters on the table. "You pick them. Play something that snaps along a little. I'm going back there to see if I can speed things up. I've got to head out to Barlow early tomorrow."

I asked for a glass of water at the counter because my throat was dry. Out on the river, a small sailboat caught the last rays of the sun, and I couldn't imagine who might be out there sailing in this desolate place.

Riley returned, his mouth set in a thin line. "I can't figure where she's got herself off to."

"Maybe she walked home," I said. "Maybe she wanted to be on her own a while."

"Darned crazy thing to do, if she did."

Riley asked the waitress to check the women's bathroom and make certain Mom hadn't fainted from the heat, but she came back out shaking her head. We hung around another half hour and Riley tried not to look at the waitress. "She didn't say anything?" he asked me.

I spread my hands. "Not to me."

Finally, Riley went outside to talk with one of the kids pumping gas. I could tell how much Riley hated doing it, because they were the kind of wise-asses you always see at gas stations — ripped jeans, dirty caps tipped back on their heads — kids just waiting to drink a couple six-packs after work.

"Saw a gal climb into a big, old Bekins moving truck and head north," one kid said. He stuffed part of a candy bar into his mouth and tossed the wrapper at the trash bucket. "I suppose that could have been her."

"Was she wearing a green dress?" Riley asked. "Sunglasses?"

"Can't say for sure," the kid said. "Wasn't looking much at the dress." Smirking now, he winked at his buddy.

"Good legs for an old gal," the buddy said.

Anger flushed my face, and even though they were a couple years older than me, I wanted for Riley and me to take them, but he let it drop.

"I'm sure that wasn't Flora," Riley said as we headed for the car. "That's not one bit like her."

The speedometer stayed under ten miles per hour all the way to Griggs. "Look sharp," he told me. "She might have took sick and be lying in the ditch somewhere. Those pears looked touched. She saw that right off. I wished she'd ordered the peaches instead."

"I'm keeping my eyes peeled, Riley," I said. And I was, but when I got to thinking about the new green dress and the sunglasses, I didn't think she was in any ditch. As we pulled off the main road and into Griggs, the Coastal Flyer came by, and I thought of the time I had ridden across the state with my mother. Now I half-wished she might be on that train, heading somewhere exciting.

As the train passed, Riley opened the car door to spit, so I spotted them first. The crossing gate was still going up, its red lights blinking, and I had to strain my eyes a little to make out the two white figures against the shadowy background of willows at the river's edge. The moon had just risen above the basalt cliffs and covered everything with an eerie, pale light.

Dwight had taken off all his clothes — including the railroad cap, but his size and shape were unmistakable, even at that distance. She was naked too, and they were in the shallows but wading toward deep water.

Riley hadn't closed the car door; his arm remained straight out from his side and seemed frozen stiff. Then he muttered, "Flora, by God."

When he looked at me, Riley's eyes were widened in amazement and confusion. I realized then that he understood nothing about his life or circumstances; chances were slim he ever would. And I believed he was capable of some desperate act, the kind you read about in newspapers.

He got out of the car, and the gravel crunched beneath his feet as he began striding toward the two waders. "Hey," he shouted, but they didn't hear him. "Hey, goddamnit!"

I climbed out too, thinking I could stop him. I slammed the car door and broke into a run, hoping I could catch up.

Kari Sharp hill

Expiration Dates

Bill had stayed around longer than any other man, even longer than the two years Emma's father spent with her. She wondered what was keeping Bill near her. The answer wasn't in the mirror. Her hair was a washed out brown, too fine to do anything with. She was fourteen pounds overweight and freckled far beyond cute.

"Men only love one thing," Emma's mother always said. Emma believed the statement but not the implication. Bill never seemed particularly driven by sex. He was a cooperative lover, lending her his body as easily as he lent her a book. Bill's "one thing" wasn't sex. Emma needed to know what it was.

"Why are you here?" Emma asked him the night following their twenty-fifth month anniversary celebration.

"You invited me." He frowned, confused, not angry. "I thought we were gonna watch a movie."

"No, I mean why are you here with me?" Emma studied his face.

"Is this a cosmetic question?"

"What?"

"Like where the planets all get in a straight row and shazam! Here we are?"

"Cosmic." Emma smiled. "No. It's nothing like that."

"I love you," he told her. "Is that the right answer?"

Emma was sure he didn't love her and that made it all the worse when he said it. She had liked it at first when Bill left a few clothes in her closet. But lately, his good suit seemed to hang too close to the end of the rack, like an empty man on the edge. The shaving kit he kept on the shelf behind the good towels was too small, travel size, Emma thought. His toothbrush leaned away from hers in the cup next to the sink.

"Men only love one thing," Emma said to herself, but she still didn't know what Bill's one thing was. Bill had eaten hundreds of meals in Emma's small apartment kitchen. On the evening of their twenty-six month anniversary Bill took Emma to a Barry Manilow concert. Late that night, after they'd made lukewarm love, Emma stood naked at the breadboard making him a sandwich. She was strictly a Miracle Whip person but Bill preferred real mayonnaise. So for the last couple of years she'd been buying both. She spread mayo on thick slices of dark rye, adding layers of shaved ham and havarti, an offering on a Dusty Rose china plate.

After Bill had eaten, he showered and went home to sleep. That's when it occurred to Emma that he might be dating her just for the convenience of a high cholesterol sandwich spread.

The mayonnaise was the first thing to go.

Emma put on her heavy robe and her boots. She carried the mayo to the garbage can outside, dropping the jar from eye level, straight as a bomb. Emma then rearranged her remaining condiments, noting the expiration date on each label.

It only took Bill a few weeks to get used to eating his sandwiches with margarine and just a touch of mustard. "Better for me," he said, but Emma wondered what this sacrifice really proved. Mayonnaise, she decided, wasn't much of a test on which to base a whole relationship. She opened the kitchen cupboards and glared at the contents. One by one, Emma broke every dish, saving a single dinner plate. She scraped her scratch-proof skillet until little beads of dangerous looking brown vinyl stuff clung to the surface of the pan. She dented pan bottoms on the bedpost of her custom antiqued bed, bent tines on the forks, hammered spoons flat and fashioned knives into boomerangs that would never come back. Emma smashed glasses. She held Tupperware over the stove burner until holes yawned in the Very Berry Blue plastic. Emma smirked at what she had once considered an impressive Lifetime Warranty on bowls that burped.

"Would you like to eat out more often?" Bill asked when he noticed the cupboards were empty. He eyed the last Tater Tot on the plate between them, then sliced it in half with their fork. Emma shrugged. After a few one-place-setting meals, Bill seemed to think sharing was romantic. "Finger food is fun," he said. "You can eat it anywhere." He winked and nodded toward the bedroom.

The next afternoon Emma sold her bed. She got a good price for it in spite of the chipped post. She gave away her sheets, the quilt her mother made, the dual-control electric blanket, her goose down pillows. At the last minute, she remembered the Hide-a-Bed lurking under the couch cushions in the living room. She pushed the sofa out into the hall and placed a "free" sign on it.

"I'm not really tired," Bill said when he noticed the bed was missing. They started staying up later. They watched old movies on cable. One movie was about Lewis and Clark. Fred MacMurray played Lewis who fell in love with Donna Reed in braids, playing Sacajawea. In the end, when Sacajawea rode out alone on the stagecoach, Emma started to cry.

Bill laughed. "It's just a movie," he said. Then he kissed her forehead. "I love watching these old films," he whispered. That night the blue scatter rug Emma dreamed on became a newly discovered river, and Bill turned into Fred MacMurray. Donna Reed unbraided her hair, put on a pretty dress, and missed the coach out of town.

The next morning Emma woke with the sad suspicion that Bill had probably stuck with her because of the thirty-two inch television and her VCR Plus. She knew men loved big TV's. Emma put the portable television in her bathtub. Then she dragged in the VCR, her boom box with a CD player, and the dual alarm clock radio. She sprinkled the electronics liberally with Calgon and turned on the water.

Emma called a moving company with same day service just before she tossed in her cordless phone. Overalled men carried out slightly damp boxes of electronics without comment. While they were there she had them load up her dining table, her Lazy Boy, and the end tables with the built-in coasters. She sent her dresser and the sewing machine on which she'd once shortened a pair of Bill's pants. They carried away Emma's smaller things in large, secret, green garbage bags. Emma wrote the men a check and sent them across five wide states with her stuff, to a fictitious address in Ohio.

The apartment was finally empty. Old water stains on the floor seemed to ache for furniture to hide them. The air felt thin with nothing to anchor it. Emma had trouble catching her breath. She leaned against a yellow wall and slid down, stretching her bare legs out in front of her. She rubbed her palm lightly across the hardwood floor.

"It's so peaceful here without all that white noise," Bill told her that night. He talked more than he ever had. He told her about growing up in a mill town, a noisy, dirty place. "All my life, I've longed for a quiet this clean," he said. "No one has ever listened to me the way you do," he told her, holding her close.

Emma broke all windows, pane by pain, to let mean noise in. She tied a scarf tight around her head until her ears were numb in the cottony quiet, until he knew she'd never hear another word he said. "You talk," he said. "I'll listen."

Bill listened too closely, as if he were waiting for some revelation she didn't have to give him. Her nonsense talk delighted him. She recited poetry to break his heart, and he thanked her. He listened so closely, she couldn't bear it. She knew Bill only stayed for the words. Emma bit her tongue until it swelled beyond language.

With nothing else to look at in the barren apartment, Bill's eyes were always on Emma. He liked to braid her hair. He stroked the thin skin of her eyelids, the curve of her ear. Bill dropped her only nightgown over her head and watched it flow down her body like warm honey.

Emma burned her clothes. She chopped her hair into nubby little clumps too short to curl. "There you are," he said as if he'd been looking for her for years.

She unscrewed the hinges that held the front door to the wall. She removed all the locks. Emma couldn't stand knowing that he stayed with her because he was trapped behind a locked door. That night, when Bill tried to open the door, it crashed into the apartment. "That's easy," he said, grinning. "Hi, Emma."

Emma closed her eyes and listened to the slide of his soft-soled shoes across her bare, scarred floor. He made long love to her, whispering beneath her. She imagined tiny floor splinters digging into his back, but he didn't complain.

When she woke, the next morning, Emma found a message he'd carved into the hardwood boards beside her. *It's your heart I love.* And the words began to ache deep in her chest.

"…it is testimony to the insidious effects of happiness on some of the greatest minds in history that some philosophers have argued that the pursuit of happiness is the ultimate aim of all human endeavors."

— Richard P. Bentall

Chuck Palahniuk

Fight Club

Two screens into my demo to Microsoft, I taste blood and have to start swallowing. My boss doesn't know the material, but he won't let me run the demo with a black eye and half my face swollen from the stitches inside my cheek. The stitches have come loose, and I can feel them with my tongue against the inside of my cheek. Picture snarled fishing line on the beach. I can picture them as the black stitches on a dog after it's fixed, and I keep swallowing blood. My boss is making the presentation from my script, and I'm running the laptop projector so I'm off to one side of the room, in the dark.

More of my lips are sticky with blood as I try to lick the blood off my lips, and when the lights come up, I will turn to consultants Ellen and Walter and Norbert and Linda from Microsoft and say, thank you for coming, my mouth shining with blood and blood climbing the cracks between my teeth.

You can swallow about a pint of blood before you're sick.

Fight club is tonight, and I'm not going to miss fight club.

Before the presentation, Walter from Microsoft smiles his steam shovel jaw like a marketing tool tanned the color of a barbecued potato chip. Walter with his signet ring shakes my hand, wrapped in his smooth soft hand and says, "I'd hate to see what happened to the other guy."

The first rule about fight club is you don't talk about fight club.
I tell Walter I fell.

Before the presentation, when I sat across from my boss, telling him where in the script each slide cues and when I wanted to run the video segment, my boss says, "What do you get yourself into every weekend?"

"I just don't want to die without a few scars," I say. It's nothing anymore to have a beautiful stock body. You see those cars that are completely stock cherry, right out of a dealer's showroom in 1955, I always think, what a waste.

The second rule about fight club is you don't talk about fight club.

Maybe at lunch, the waiter comes to your table and the waiter has the two black eyes of a giant panda from fight club last weekend when you saw him get his head pinched between the concrete floor and the knee of a two-hundred-pound stock boy who kept slamming a fist into the bridge of the waiter's nose again and again in flat hard-packing sounds you could hear over all the yelling until the waiter caught enough breath and sprayed blood to say, stop.

You don't say anything because fight club exists only in the hours between when fight club starts and when fight club ends.

You saw the kid who works in the copy center, a month ago you saw this kid who can't remember to three-hole punch an order or put colored slip sheets between the copy packets, but this kid was a god for ten minutes when you saw him kick the air out of an account representative twice his size, then land on the man and pound him limp until the kid had to stop. That's the third rule in fight club, when someone says stop, or goes limp, even if he's just faking it, the fight is over. Every time you see this kid, you can't tell him what a great fight he had.

Only two guys to a fight. One fight at a time. They fight without shirts or shoes. The fights go on as long as they have to. Those are the other rules of fight club.

Who guys are in fight club is not who they are in the real world. Even if you told the kid in the copy center that he had a good fight, you wouldn't be talking to the same man.

After a night in fight club, everything in the real world gets the volume turned down. Nothing can piss you off. Your word is law, and if other people break that law or question you, even that doesn't piss you off.

In the real world, I'm an on-site campaign coordinator in a shirt and tie, sitting in the dark with a mouthful of blood and changing the overheads and slides as my boss tells Microsoft how he chose a particular shade of pale cornflower blue for an icon.

The first fight club was just Tyler and me pounding on each other.

It used to be enough that when I came home angry and knowing that my life wasn't toeing my five-year plan, I used to clean my condominium or detail my car. Someday I'd be dead without a scar and there would be a really nice condo and car. Really, really nice, until the dust settled or the next owner. Nothing is static. Even the Mona Lisa is falling apart. Since fight club, I can wiggle half the teeth in my jaw.

Tyler never knew his father.

Tyler and I still go to fight club, together. Fight club is in the basement of a bar, now, after the bar closes on Saturday night, and every week you go and there's more guys there.

Tyler gets under the one light in the middle of the black concrete basement and he can see that light flickering back out of the dark in a hundred pairs of eyes. First thing Tyler yells is, "The first rule about fight club is you don't talk about fight club."

"The second rule about fight club," Tyler yells, "is you don't talk about fight club."

Me, I knew my dad for about six years, but I don't remember anything. My dad, he starts a new family in a new town about every six years. This isn't so much like a family as it's like he sets up a franchise.

What you see at fight club is a generation of men raised by women.

Tyler standing under the one light in the after-midnight blackness of a basement full of men, Tyler runs through the other rules: two men per fight, one fight at a time, no shoes no shirts, fights go on as long as they have to.

"And the seventh rule," Tyler yells, "is if this is your first night at fight club, you have to fight."

Fight club is not football on television. You aren't watching a bunch of men you don't know halfway around the world beating on each other live by satellite with a two-minute delay, commercials every ten minutes, and a pause now for station identification. After you've been to fight club, watching football on television is watching pornography when you could be having great sex. Fight club gets to be your reason for going to the gym and keeping your hair cut short and cutting your nails. The gyms you go to are crowded with guys trying to look like men, as if being a man means looking the way a sculptor or an art director says. Like Tyler says, even a soufflé looks big.

My father never went to college so it was really important I go to college. After college, I called him long distance and said, "Now what?" My dad didn't know. When I got a job and turned twenty-five, long distance I said "Now what?" My dad didn't know. So he said, get married.

I'm a twenty-five-year-old boy, and I'm wondering if another woman is really the answer I need.

What happens at fight club doesn't happen in words. Some guys need a fight every week. This week Tyler says it's the first fifty guys through the door and that's it. No more.

Last week, I tapped a guy and he and I got on the list for a fight. This guy must've had a bad week, got both my arms behind my head in a full nelson and rammed my face into the concrete floor until my teeth bit open the inside of my cheek and my eye swelled shut and was bleeding, and after I said, stop, I could look down and there was a print of half my face in blood on the floor.

Tyler stood next to me, both of us looking down at the big O of my mouth with blood all around it and the little slit of my eye staring up at us from the floor, and Tyler says, "Cool."

I shake the guy's hand and say, "Good fight."

This guy, he says, "How about next week?"

I try to smile against all the swelling, and I say, "Look at me. How about next month?"

You aren't alive anywhere like you're alive at fight club. When it's you and one other guy under that one light in the middle of all those watching. Fight club isn't about winning or losing fights. Fight club isn't about words. You see a guy come to fight club for the first time, and his ass is a loaf of white bread. You see this same guy here six months later, and he looks carved out of wood. This guy trusts himself to handle anything. There's grunting and noise at fight club like at the gym, but fight club isn't about looking good. There's hysterical shouting in tongues like at church, and when you wake up Sunday afternoon you feel saved.

After my last fight, the guy who fought me mopped the floor while I called my insurance to pre-approve a visit to the emergency room. At the hospital, Tyler tells them I fell down. Outside, the sun was coming up.

You don't talk about fight club because except for five hours from two until seven on Sunday morning, fight club doesn't exist.

When we invented fight club, Tyler and I, neither of us had ever been in a fight before. If you've never been in a fight, you wonder. About getting hurt, about what you're capable of doing against another man. I was the first guy Tyler ever felt safe enough to ask, and we were both drunk in a bar where no one would care so Tyler said, "I want you to do me a favor. I want you to hit me as hard as you can."

I didn't want to, but Tyler explained it all, about not wanting to die without any scars, about being tired of watching only professionals fight, and wanting to know more about himself. At the time, Tyler's life just seemed too complete, and maybe we have to break everything to make something better out of ourselves.

I looked around, okay, I said, but outside in the parking lot.

So we went outside, and I asked if Tyler wanted it in the face or in the stomach.

Tyler said, "Surprise me."

I said I'd never hit anybody.

Tyler said, "So go crazy, man."

I said, "Close your eyes."

Tyler said, "No."

Like every guy on his first night in fight club, I breathed in and swung my fist in a roundhouse at Tyler's jaw like in every cowboy movie we'd ever seen, and me, my fist connected with the side of Tyler's neck.

"Shit," I said, "that didn't count. I want to try it again."

Tyler said, yeah it counted, and hit me, straight on, pow, just like a cartoon boxing glove on a spring on Saturday morning cartoons, right in the middle of my chest and I fell back against a car. We both stood there, Tyler rubbing the side of his neck and me holding a hand on my chest, both of us knowing we'd gotten somewhere we'd never been and like the cat and mouse in cartoons, we were still alive and wanted to see how far we could take this thing and still be alive.

Tyler said, "Cool."

I said, "Hit me again."

Tyler said, "No, you hit me.

So I hit him, a girl's wide roundhouse to right under his ear, and Tyler shoved me back and stomped the heel of his shoe in my stomach. What happened next and after that didn't happen in words, but the bar closed and people came out and shouted around us in the parking lot.

Instead of Tyler, I felt finally I could get my hands on everything in the world that didn't work, my cleaning that came back with the collar buttons broken, the bank that says I'm short two hundred dollars. My job where my boss got on my computer and fiddled with my DOS execute commands. And Marla. Nothing was solved when the fight was over, but nothing mattered.

This was a Sunday night and Tyler hadn't shaved all weekend, so my knuckles burned raw from his weekend beard. Us lying on our backs in the parking lot, staring up at the one star that came through the street lights, I asked Tyler what he'd been fighting.

Tyler said, his father.

Maybe we didn't need a father to complete ourselves. There's nothing personal about who you fight in fight club. You fight to fight. You're not supposed to talk about fight club, but we talked and for the rest of the summer, guys met in that parking lot after the bar had closed, and by the time it got cold, another bar offered the basement where we meet now.

When fight club meets, Tyler gives the rules he and I decided. "Most of you," Tyler yells in the cone of light in the center of the basement full of men, "you're here because someone broke the rules. Somebody told you about fight club."

Tyler says, "Well, you better stop talking or you'd better start another fight club because next week you put your name on a list when you get here, and only the first fifty names on the list get in. If you get in, you set up your fight right away if you want a fight. If you don't want a fight, there are guys who do, so maybe you should just stay home.

"If this is your first night at fight club," Tyler yells, "you have to fight."

Most guys are at fight club because of something they're too scared to fight. After a few fights, you're afraid of a lot less.

A lot of best friends meet for the first time at fight club. Anymore, I go to meetings or conferences and see faces at conferences tables, accountants and junior executives or attorneys with broken noses spreading out like an eggplant under the edges of bandages or they have a couple stitches under an eye or a jaw wired shut. These are quiet young men who listen until it's time to decide. We nod to each other. Later, my boss will ask me how I know so many of these guys.

According to my boss, there are fewer and fewer gentlemen in business and more thugs.

The demo goes on.

Walter from Microsoft catches my eye. Here's a young guy with perfect teeth and clear skin and the kind of job you bother to write the alumni magazine about getting. You know he was too young to fight in any wars, and if his parents weren't divorced, his father was never home, and here he's looking at me with half my face clean shaved and half a leering bruise hidden in the dark. Blood shining on my lips. And maybe Walter's thinking about a meatless, pain-free potluck he went to last weekend or the ozone or the Earth's desperate need to stop cruel product testing on animals, but probably he's not.

Joanne B. Mulcahy

Dreams of Martyrdom

Driving south along the Willamette River to my home in Portland, I saw a crowd gathered on the river bank just above a row of houseboats. A series of ripples in the water, an arm gesturing for help. I parked the car and scrambled down the steep incline to the water's edge. As I moved through the crowd, people moved aside, recognizing the certainty of my mission. I pulled my sweater overhead, kicked off my shoes, and dove. Sinking deep into the murky water, moving towards the figure fighting against the current, I heard a call from childhood. A clear echo of Sister Peter Eileen's voice reverberating through the black water: "The only happiness is in sacrifice for others." Putting aside fear, I groped towards the upturned hand of the drowning man. One hand cupped under his chin, I struggled with the other arm towards shore. Coughing and spitting, I began to sink under his incessant pull. A light shone above me as I went down down, released into the ultimate state of grace: martyrdom.

 But that's not how it happened. I didn't stop; I never even slowed down. I read later that a scull had overturned. Another boat picked up the rower and the crowd dispersed within minutes, while I, worried about getting to the grocery store, anxious about the forty papers I had yet to grade, continued on. But not without a fantasy, one that takes over with such speed and clings with such tenacity that I've come to recognize it as a reflex.

In the fantasy, I am a savior. I am graceful and strong. I'm flying, sometimes swimming, always with the natural fluidity of an athlete. With little thought for myself, I wildly risk all for the sake of…who? In purer days, I saved old people and animals. Then adolescence. For an embarrassingly long period, I longed to rescue young (rich and available) men, future romantic partners. Thankfully, with time and maturity, my fantasies shifted to computer salesmen who reward me with the laptop I so covet. Pathetic, even sinful, Sister Peter Eileen would say, layering my transgressions upon one another: coveting thy neighbor's goods, fantasizing sexual encounters (in Catholicism, even desire is a sin), and worst of all, striving for personal gain. Happiness can only be attained through sacrifice; and sacrifice only counts if it's pure.

I wasn't always so brazen and unorthodox in my desires. In fifth grade, I longed to give selflessly. I stood ready to offer all that I had for Father Devrees. My chance came on the first Friday afternoon of Lent, the month-long ritual preparation for Easter. The sisters at St. Ursula's elementary school outside Philadelphia hurried us through morning lessons with *The Baltimore Catechism* to allow for a full, free afternoon. The recitations of "Who made me? God made me" primed us for my favorite Lenten ritual, the stations of the cross. After lunch, we abandoned the odor of linoleum and the faded brick of our worn schoolhouse for the gleaming white steeple and pungent incense of the stately church next door. I moved, eyes downcast, silently praying through the stations, the fourteen pictures that carried me along Christ's journey to his crucifixion. "Jesus receives the Cross. Jesus falls for the first time. Jesus is met by his blessed mother." I always hurried to the sixth station, the meeting with St. Veronica where the impression of Christ's face imprints the cloth she brings for him to wipe away the sweat. I lingered at the final station where Christ's body is lowered from the cross, blood flowing from hands and feet. Each image transported me further into the world of barefoot, white-robed, suffering Christians. Shrouds, crowns of thorns, bloodied bodies hung in agony. A world of sacred violence.

I loved the silence, the meditation, the slow, even quality of those afternoons. I didn't even mind missing vocal, our usual Friday activity. Since the school couldn't afford musical instruments, vocal was our compromise. For twenty-five cents, we passed Friday afternoons singing show tunes with the sisters. Memories of *Oklahoma* and *South Pacific* now merge with the ritual of the stations. The smiling, voluptuous image of Mary Martin on the *South Pacific* album cover melds with the station where Christ meets the women of Jerusalem. I hear St. Veronica singing "I'm gonna wash that man right out of my hair." Sacrilege, you might think, but something else alchemized on those afternoons, a naive mix of secular and sacred. In our Irish-Italian neighborhood, where a walk to the nearby sewage plant on Darby Creek was a wilderness adventure, where rummage sales and bridge parties comprised social life, religion offered vistas at least as exotic as the South Pacific. Once a week, Bali Hai and heaven merged in our suburban Philadelphia enclave. I loved Friday afternoons.

On this particular Friday, we waited in our seats for Sister to announce the lines for church. John Moriarty, the scourge of the classroom, sat in front of me, pounding on the desk, eager to leap from his seat and be first in line. I hated sitting behind him. I feared touching the dandruff that settled on the greasy collar of his maroon uniform jacket. When Sister Eileen finally entered the room, a hush descended. "Class, we will not begin our stations today as scheduled. God has another plan for us." I cringed, fearful this plan might entail more time behind John Moriarty. Instead, Sister ushered the girls out into the dark hallway in single file. Uniform check, I thought. As usual, she'd run a yardstick along the bottom edges of our skirts, calculating length and ensuring modesty. But this day was to be different. We had a mission.

"We'll begin with you girls," said Sister. "Each of you has a special gift of sight given by God." This, we knew. We heard stories almost hourly about those less fortunate than us — lepers, the blind, the maimed, and unluckiest of all, communists. Unlike the godless communists, we knew we were blessed. Sighted, baptized, with full use of our limbs, and most important, Americans free to sacrifice our way to happiness. An additional message — implicit, never spoken

— fueled our drive: as girls, we were especially suited to sacrifice. "We'll use that sight today, girls, to help us in our search." Mystified, we moved out into the schoolyard, then onto the large lawn that separated the school from the red brick church and rectory. Sister Eileen towered imposingly before us. "Our mission, class, is to find Father Devrees' finger." A collective gasp rose. I conjured up an image of Father Devrees. Of slight build, with dark, wavy, thick hair and penetrating blue eyes, Father Devrees was our newest and youngest priest, recently arrived from Russia or some Eastern European country. (My mother now tells me that his name was Decrees, and that he was Belgian. But I knew better; there is no place on the map of godless communism for Belgium.)

I was in love with Father Devrees. All the girls were. With his carefully trimmed goatee, he was an exotic, clerical Mitch Miller. I scanned the yard and beyond to the rectory. The real Father was nowhere in sight. That, Sister Eileen explained, was because he had his hand wrapped, awaiting the discovery of the finger he had cut off trying to fix the lawn mower. God was cruel to have maimed Father Devrees during such a mundane pursuit. But I would find the finger. Or I would give my own. Through suffering and sacrifice, happiness would be mine.

My fifth-grade class of sixty made a formidable search team. Sister Eileen followed us outside with the boys. We formed five lines of twelve and began to move in single file, eyes fixed upon the ground. I remembered reading about the pilgrims who prayed continuously, and began a mantra that directed my breathing, "Please, God, the finger." It became simply, "The Finger." I had never prayed so intently. Tempted to wander off on my own, I steeled myself to stay close to the line of uniformed girls. My grade in self-control had slipped on the last report card. Earlier in the year, when President Kennedy was assassinated, my faith had wavered. Questions stacked up. How could Father, Son, and Holy Ghost be one? Why didn't the Virgin Mary get in on the Holy Trinity? Was everything a mystery? Here was the chance to strengthen my faith. Surely, adherence to Sister's orders, endless devotion, and my deep desire to sacrifice would bring me to the finger.

Pacing tirelessly, I imagined the sweat on my brow wiped by St. Veronica's cloth. I mentally braced myself to cut off my own finger if I didn't find Father Devrees' lost digit. I imagined fingers floating in the air before me. The repetition of my footsteps echoed my mantra. I fell into a trance state, walking, praying, walking, then suddenly, a gleam of flesh. I looked down at the stub nearly buried in the newly cut grass. Undisturbed by the sight of blood, which normally sickened me, I picked up the finger and ran to the rectory, crying out to Father Devrees that he was saved. I had found the finger. He came out, his bloody stub bound in rags. I looked deeply into Father Devrees' eyes, certain of his undying devotion. Because I had been willing to selflessly sacrifice, happiness would be ours. We got down on our knees and thanked God for our sight, our belief, our freedom, and miracles. It was my moment of glory.

But that's not how it happened. John Moriarty found the finger. And I was then and forever certain that there was no God. Or if he existed, he was a Protestant. Despite what the nuns had told us, I couldn't believe in the existence of a Catholic God that would allow the greasy, hell-raising John Moriarty to find the finger. He was a boy; what did he know about sacrifice? Even Sister Eileen looked disappointed. Her narrow face, imprisoned by the white headdress of her habit, drooped further as she moved to investigate the cries of glee in the far corner of the rectory lawn. John was shouting and waving wildly, "I've got it, I've got it!" "This is not a football game, John," Sister proclaimed as she ran, the black robes of her habit flowing in the wind behind her, to retrieve the finger. She carried it to the rectory, and we all watched as Father Devrees walked out to the car to be driven to St. Luke's Hospital, where the Sisters of Mercy would attend to the bloody digit, now on ice. There would be prayers and reaffirmations of belief. Father Devrees would return grateful for full use of his appendage, and of course, his freedom.

When the commotion died down, and Sister led us back to the classroom, I pondered the meaning of the afternoon's events. If freedom and faith meant that John Moriarty could triumph on this fine spring day, I wondered if I wasn't destined for the land of godless communism. Nothing made sense anymore. I had not found the finger. I had not had the chance to sacrifice myself. And we had missed vocal *and* the stations of the cross.

The teachings encased in three books dominated my education at St. Ursula's. I remember each by its color — green, blue, and yellow. The three texts combined with inklike permanency to shape the story of who I would become. We began each day with prayers from the green book, *The Baltimore Catechism*. As I walked to school across the empty lot behind our street, I practiced recitations for the day. "God made me to know him, to love him, and to serve him in this world." The mantra burrowed into the unconscious. "Service" was the operative world. Doing for others was the path to heaven. Not to "serve" was "selfish," a term delivered with a mixture of scorn and pity, spit out rather than stated. A rival epithet was "conceited," particularly damning for girls. "Full of herself," I once heard Sister Eileen sniff to one of the other sisters, tossing her black-robed arm toward curly-haired Dawn Montgomery, the most beautiful girl in the class. I suspected the scorn for Dawn rose from her status as the only non-Catholic in the school. Her soul was damned. But worse, she was "full of herself." She would never learn to serve.

Morning prayers were followed by readings from the big blue book, *Lives of The Saints*, that Sister Eileen kept high up on a shelf. Only the best readers were chosen to deliver a saint's story for the day. I longed to be chosen to read about my favorite saints. St. Joan of Arc, the star martyr, dizzying in her bravery, mysteriously androgynous. My namesake saint. Her picture in the blue book stays imprinted in memory: Joan resplendent in white, straight backed, leading the French army on horseback to the siege of Orleans. Joan enveloped by leaping flames after capture by the English and her refusal to denounce the saints who had directed her to battle. St. Ava, who when thrown to the lions, remained curiously untouched. Terese of Liseux. Not one of the great martyrs, her health precluded extreme suffering, but she endured each day by creating small trials which she recorded in *The Story of a Soul*. The blue book listed the French title, *L'Histoire*

D'une Ame, in parentheses. I mouthed the words over and over, drawn in by the exotic sounds and by Terese's persona as a "small martyr." Though I longed for the glamour of martyrdom, secretly, I recoiled at the thought of too much hardship.

Near the end of fifth grade, after Easter had passed, my disappointment over the finger episode lingered. I wondered if I would ever regain my faith and belief in suffering. In late spring, the sisters introduced us to a world of potential sacrifice for all Catholic girls. On a Saturday trip to the Waverly theater, we saw enacted on the big screen a story unforgettable for those of us entering adolescence in the early 1960s: the life of St. Maria Goretti. An Italian peasant girl murdered at the turn of the century by a youth inflamed with lustful desire, Maria died of multiple stab wounds in defense of her chastity. Here was a test of faith that many of us would face, sister stated without further elaboration. Since I knew nothing of peasants and less about sex, the real meaning of Maria's story eluded me. But the Italian girls in my neighborhood took on a special glow. A glimmer of faith had been rekindled.

For the remainder of fifth grade, our class made weekly visits to the sixth-grade room where Helen Pineau offered French instruction from the 1950 RCA television the sisters rolled up from the convent on a wheeled tray. After French lessons, I would walk home down to Darby Creek. In the privacy of the woods, I practiced my pronunciations of "Liseaux," "Jeanne D'Arc" (I had discovered St. Joan's "real" name), and *L'Historie D'Une Ame*. I pulled down the sides of my mouth, searched for the guttural "r's" in the back of my throat, mimicking Helen Pineau's tortured movements. As I rounded the end of the creek path and headed home, I could smell garlic wafting from the kitchens of our Italian neighbors. Groaning out French sounds, longing for the everyday exotica of spaghetti dinners, I knew only this: that the path to sainthood was bound up with being French like St. Terese or Italian like St. Maria, with being something other than Irish, someone other than me. The someone I might be if I discovered the right sacrifice, if I could somehow suffer enough.

In sixth grade, a new sister arrived at St. Ursula's with a steeled devotion to discipline and a passion for early Christian history. With her came the yellow, bible study book whose stories came to haunt me. I still see the faded yellow cover, worn by children's hands, stained from dirty fingers. The stories within detailed the suffering of the third-century Christians forced underground to worship, only to be discovered and thrown to the lions by the Roman soldiers. The illustrations highlighted the horror: faces frozen in terror, human forms hurled into the Coliseum, the aftermath of mangled bodies. The thought of the catacombs made me claustrophobic; worse, I could no longer imagine martyrdom without gore.

During recess after bible study one day, I approached Sister Mary Cyril. "Sister, that could never happen again, could it, the lions and everything?" I asked, a plea for reassurance swelling through my tone. Sister turned to her desk drawer, her face solemn. She took out a photograph. The picture showed emaciated adults in prisonlike settings, their grim visages a modern-day version of faces in the yellow, bible study book. "*When* do you think these people lived?" she queried. "Long ago?" I offered hopefully. Sister narrowed her eyes. "Today," she pronounced definitively. "And *where* do you think they live?" I was stuck. "The ghetto?" I puzzled, evoking that generic place of poverty, sin, and tragedy from which we, in the blessed suburbs, were gratefully shielded. "No, dear," she returned wearily, "these unfortunate people live in Russia, where they are dying for their faith. Krushchev is the evil man responsible." I already knew about Eastern Europe from my John Nagy "Learn to Draw" sketches of Hungarian refugees. But Russia. An unimaginable place, worse than the Coliseum and the ghetto combined. Russians. They triggered both fear and the deep allure of the forbidden. Krushchev. The Devil Incarnate, destroyer of children and Christians. The Roman emperor of our age, his land the modern Coliseum. The innocent days of St. Veronica singing songs from *South Pacific* gave way to fear of lustful men with knives, the jaws of the lions, Krushchev and his henchmen. No matter which way you turned, there was no shortage of tortures to endure. Suffering began to lose its sheen.

When I entered junior high school, my parents decided on a seismic shift in our education. My sister Pat had developed a stomach ulcer which my parents attributed to Catholic schools. We went "public," as we referred to our neighbors who attended nonparochial schools. We had often wondered what became of their wayward, non-Catholic souls; now, we joined their ranks. At first, thin and shy, I hopped to my feet when called upon by the teacher, face flushed at my inability to lose the trappings of obedience and conformity Catholic school had drilled into me. But I acculturated quickly. By eighth grade, I lingered in the bathroom after study hall, drawn by the girls in miniskirts and boots, thick black eyeliner on shaded lids, blowing Marlboro smoke through whitened lips. Sirenlike, they called to me with their smoky conversation of boys and shoplifting on Saturdays. Like Dawn Montgomery, they didn't care that their souls were damned. I yearned to be like them. Beyond the need to be good, freed from the thirst for salvation.

Through junior high and into high school, I skipped classes to smoke in the bathroom. Left alone, I read. My record was *Franny and Zooey*, *Catcher in the Rye*, and a pack of Marlboros, in the same stall on a single day. I consumed most of French class there, reading Baudelaire and Rimbaud from a big, blue book that bore a striking resemblance to *Lives of the Saints*. I went into hiding once again as I tortured my mouth into French pronunciation, longing for an identity more exotic than my own. Abandoning my quest for a holy self, I searched for another in a world of new books.

By my junior year, the bathroom stalls had grown risky. I spent most of my time looking for other places to spend my school hours undetected. One day, I pretended to leave for school and walked instead to the library of a small local college. There, in the basement of the building, I discovered an empty study room marked "smoking." Inside, a long oval table full of ashtrays stood surrounded by walls of leather-bound books. I lit a Marlboro and pulled one of the worn volumes off the shelf. I ran my fingers along the gold inlay on the blood-red leather. *Crime and Punishment* by Fyodor Dostoevsky. My body twitched with anticipation and desire. I reached further and yanked down one book after another. Pushkin, Tolstoy, Turgenev. Russians! A surge of surprise and pleasure — the deep thrill of forbidden fruit. A world cordoned off to me from childhood.

Stroking the finely tooled leather, I settled down to read, beginning with Dostoevsky. I worked from *Crime and Punishment* into *The Idiot, The Brothers Karamazov, Notes From Underground,* and other stories. I plunged deep, flirting with the dangerous, enticing edges of Dostoevskian contradiction. Saintly prostitutes. "Meek" women with steel determination who longed to rescue doomed outsiders. Dark characters like Raskolnikov who committed murder to save the world. Gamblers, drunks, and murderers, beating their brows, pacing underground, self-lacerating, longing for pain, hungering for redemption. Characters built on paradox, every dark pursuit yielding a new self. Their journeys repelled and fascinated me at the same time. Just like the mysteries of religion. I heard Sister Eileen's voice. "Happiness through suffering." Terrifyingly familiar ground.

I turned to Tolstoy, moving from *Ann Karenina* to *War and Peace.* The female characters gripped me. I became the wildly romantic Anna, lost in the world of illicit romance and sex. In Anna, I embraced all that the sisters derided: selfishness, abandon, and carnal desire. I heaped scorn on Kitty, who lived for the happiness of others, for the fulfillment of family life — the very embodiment of the Catholic ideal. Who wanted her dull fate, built on destruction of the self, denial of the body? Maria Gorettti be damned. Freed from the confining stories of the big green, blue, and yellow books, I entered the leather-bound world of wickedness and abandon.

But that's not how it happened. At least not completely. I did flirt with rebellion. I did love the wild and romantic Russian women characters. But in the end, I could not escape my deadly attraction to Dostoevsky's "meek ones," the self-sacrificing women who gave their energies to others. Theirs was the narrative of happiness for which I'd been groomed. I read and reread *Anna Karenina,* yearning to be Anna. Instead, I felt destined to the fate of self-sacrificing Kitty. Sunk into my teenage rebellion, seemingly light-years beyond the Catholic world I longed to escape, I saw its trappings surface in the stories that continued to mold me.

I haven't re-read Russian novels for nearly twenty years. I devour biographies of women. Unambiguous tales of strong, female characters who shape their own path toward happiness. I banish heroines with self-sacrificing tendencies. But as I drove home along the Willamette River and felt the old story resurface, I wondered what it would take to dislodge the narrative of happiness through suffering. Almost immediately, I questioned what might replace it. If the stories of sacrifice proved unsatisfying and dangerous, so too did the self-absorption of characters like Anna Karenina. In the end, Anna K. self-destructed, flung across the cold iron tracks of a desolate Russian railroad station. Another version of the martyrdom story, one unredeemed by a higher purpose and thus even more unsavory.

What might be a new story to live by, an avenue toward fulfillment that neither negates nor glorifies the self? To imagine its contours, I begin with a revision of my past. I'm back at St. Ursula's searching for the finger. I no longer walk in single file. Forget self-control. Eyes wide open, I follow my intuition about the finger, careening in a jagged line across the rectory lawn. I know where the finger lies. Sister Eileen tries to call me back. John Moriarty tries to follow. But I, certain of my path, risk their anger and reproach. Midway across the lawn, I stop before the finger, wrap it in my beanie cap, and return it to Sister Eileen. John Moriarty is fuming. Father Devrees is relieved. All the other girls are proud. A victory for following one's vision, for stepping out of line in pursuit of a just cause.

What I want for young girls coming of age is the freedom to envision new stories. Then, who knows what might really happen?

Carolyn Reynolds Miller

Fugue in Green

Every day the furred green worm inside
warming the chrysalis
works out with weights
His last thrust
could light up a forest
     la luna vampira
      sexual on flowers

So spring comes crowbar and bloom
tipping the fir trees
turpentine green

     You're growing up the gray doctor said
     his hands leafed out
      twigging her branches
What could she ask
dumbbell, decibel-clumsy

why boys are taller than seaweed
and given to one-handed steering?
why they follow a green noise
     tires make against pavement

why their mouths are thistlegrin
    a girl's two-fingered whistle

Piccolo green, he pulled her down
a kiss for a penny
She heard the copperhead clink

    She wants green smoke, green silk
    a ring if
    the moon had a finger

        Ocean floor, mother of green
        scattered with shark's teeth
        gravity lives where nothing can crush it
        neither the wolf eel   nor lord turtle
        humped over the murkhole

His touch was fresher than haycock
greener than grapple

Plumb bob, green nail
she in carapace, he in green armor
unfold a house made of hinges
    spring's slow motion stem
    enters the bung-hole

    maidenhair, stag fern, applegreen gash
    worm in the apple   she remembers
    the fig tree
        didn't give a good green damn

Dressing, undressing, spring comes dicotyledon
back and forth across fields, lime-green

hypnofixing leafhopper beetles
buzzing clover's green swarm

It enters old men and sends them whacking
They lean on its wickerwood cane
because the world is in meadow

What to do with boyish clamor
a woman's evergreen body?

The moon is shoehorn green!
moonmaple slips at the window, wands

that buckle the knee or make the legs shaky
so lovers lie down for the drummer's green brush
———

Wrap-around, the skirt had a certain
hollyhock flair that couldn't be hobbled

Even dressed in curmudgeon/crabstick/crosspatch,
green would bob October for apples

    This is desire   a crone   prong green
    from the horny toad of submission
    could break her cudgel
    twitching for water
    the smell of green roses

"I feel idiotically happy today."

Drawing by Booth; © 1975
The New Yorker Magazine, Inc.

Notes on the authors

Richard P. Bentall is senior lecturer in the Department of Clinical Psychology, the University of Liverpool, England.

Marvin Bell is the author of thirteen books, most recently *The Book of the Dead Man* (poems) and *A Marvin Bell Reader* (selected poems, journals, memoirs, essays). Born in New York City, he grew up in Center Moriches, a small town on eastern Long Island. He divides his year among three locations: rural Long Island, to which he returns for six weeks each winter; Iowa City, Iowa, where he is a longtime member of the faculty of the Writers' Workshop; and Port Townsend, Washington, to which he retreats for long summers. Marvin's first book received the Lamont Award from the Academy of American Poets and in 1994 he received an Award in Literature from the American Academy of Arts and Letters.

George Booth, cartoonist, grew up in Missouri and served in the Marines where his career as a cartoonist began. He later attended various schools including the Chicago Academy of Fine Arts and the Corcoran Art School. For the past two-plus decades, George has been drawing cartoons for *The New Yorker* magazine.

Omar S. Castañeda is the Guatemalan-American author of *Remembering to Say 'Mouth' or 'Face,' Imagining Isabel, Abuela's Weave*, and other books. He teaches at Western Washington University. A writer for children, young adults, and adults, his work has received many awards.

Heather Doran Barbieri is a Seattle-based journalist, fiction writer, and poet who has published in regional and national periodicals. "Spirit Tree" is part of a short story collection funded by a grant from the Seattle Arts Commission.

Sergio Duarte Méndez was born in Guatemala in 1950. He graduated with a degree in Architecture from Universidad de San Carlos de Guatemala and also trained in film production in Madrid. He has worked as a illustrator and production manager for educational materials in Guatemala, Spain, Mexico, and Nicaragua.

Garrett Hongo's new book, *Volcano: A Memoir of Hawai'i* is out May 1995 from Alfred A. Knopf. He is professor of creative writing at the University of Oregon.

Mark Anthony Jarman, a graduate of the Iowa Writers Workshop, lives in Victoria, B.C. He is the author of *Dancing Nightly in the Tavern*, a collection of stories; *Killing the Swan*, poetry; and editor of an anthology, *Ounce of Cure*, published by Beach Holme.

Craig Lesley is the author of three novels, *Winterkill, River Song*, and *The Sky Fisherman* (Houghton Mifflin) from which his piece here is taken. He is the editor of *Talking Leaves: Contemporary Native American Short Stories*, and co-editor with his wife, Katheryn Stavrakis, of *Dreamers and Desperadoes, Contemporary Short Fiction of the American West*. Craig has received the Western Writers of America Golden Spur Award for Best Novel of the Year, and been the recipient of a National Endowment for the Arts fellowship as well as two National Endowment for the Humanities fellowships to study Native American literature. He teaches creative writing at the college level.

Lou Masson, a transplant from the Northeast, has lived in the Northwest long enough to raise three native-born Oregonians. For many years he has been a professor of literature at the University of Portland and found time to practice what he teaches as contributing editor for *Portland*. Lou's essays for that magazine have been honored with medal awards by the Council for the Advancement and Support of Education. His writing has most recently been published in *America, The Critic, Oregon East*, and *West Wind Review*.

Carolyn Reynolds Miller: "I have spent the last thirty-two years in Salem, Oregon, raising children, teaching mathematics and taking long walks. Writing is one of the long walks I enjoy. Previous publications include *Poetry Northwest, Cutbank, Hubbub*, and *Colorado Review*."

Jacqueline Moreau's photographs about mid-Columbia River Indians have toured Oregon and Washington and are used for education about Native Americans. She lives in White Salmon, Washington, with her two children, and works summers as a forest fire lookout. She has freelanced for Oregon newspapers and United Press International. Currently Jacqueline is completing a Washington State Humanities grant project, a touring exhibition sponsored by the Yakama Nation museum in Toppenish, Washington.

Joanne B. Mulcahy, a folklorist and writer, teaches at Lewis and Clark College in Portland, Oregon. Her work has appeared in *Alaska Native Magazine, Hurricane Alice, Oregon Humanities, Oregon History*, and in several anthologies, including *The Stories that Shape Us: Contemporary Women Write about the West* (W.W. Norton, 1995). She is currently writing a memoir about her experiences in Alaska.

John Nichols was born in 1940 and has lived in Taos, NM since 1969. He has published nine novels and six works of nonfiction. John is also a screenwriter and photographer.

Chuck Palahniuk (pronounced paul-ah-nik) is a thirty-two-year-old Caucasian male, five-foot-eleven, one hundred ninety pounds, brown, green. Of French and Russian descent, he is attributed to Carol and Fred Palahniuk. He has no distinguishing marks.

Bill Plympton, born in Portland, Oregon, now lives in New York City. His cartoons have appeared in *Penthouse, Rolling Stone, National Lampoon*, and *Glamour*. His first live action feature, *J. Lyle*, comes on the tail of his critically acclaimed animated musical, *The Tune*. Bill's short films have been seen widely around the country in animation festivals, and he has produced commercials for Trivial Pursuit and Sugar Delight. He has just finished a short film *Nosehair* that was in Sundance Film Festival and is starting a new animated feature called *I Married a Strange Person* due in 1997.

Lynda Sexson teaches religious studies at Montana State University. She is the author of *Ordinarily Sacred* and *Margaret of the Imperfections*. Lynda is working on a collection of stories and a novel.

Kari Sharp hill: "I was born in Washington state and I've lived here all my life but for the past few years I've spent a lot of time at an undisclosed address inside my head. There's a place there where my characters lounge on deep couches and sip unlimited quantities of Diet Coke. They wait for me to pay attention to them and sometimes they grow impatient, cooking up their own plots or whispering secrets so they can stretch out on a thick, white page. I'm fascinated by human extremes and exaggerations and the creative lengths we'll reach for to drive ourselves a little crazy. The PEN Syndication project picked up one of my stories and I was a 1991 FishTrap Fellow."

Nadja Tesich was born in Yugoslavia and worked in different areas of the film world as an actress, technician, and writer/director of her own works.

Her first play, *After The Revolution*, was produced by the Women's Project at the American Place Theatre. Nadja has received awards for "Film for My Son," a PBS award for screen writing, and a National Endowment for the Arts award for literature. Her first novel, *Shadow Partisan*, was published in 1989 by New Rivers Press, and two other novels, *Far from Vietnam* and *Native Land* are being shown to publishers. "Mothers" is excerpted from the latter, which takes place in Yugoslavia two months before the civil war. Anna, a professor of theater in New York, married and mother of two sons, goes to a conference in Dubrovnik but she stays for reasons that are not immediately clear. The book becomes a search for a missing, forgotten self, while around her the country mirrors her state and everything is ready to explode.

LEFT BANK BOOKS
A NEW WAY TO READ BETWEEN THE LINES

WRITING & FISHING THE NORTHWEST — Consider the cast. Wallace Stegner, Greg Bear, Craig Lesley, Sharon Doubiago, Nancy Lord, John Keeble. #1. ISBN 0-936085-19-3; $7.95.

EXTINCTION — Get it before it's gone. David Suzuki introduces Tess Gallagher, Barry Lopez, David Quammen, Sallie Tisdale, Robert Michael Pyle, John Callahan, Nancy Lord, and others. #2. ISBN 0-936085-50-9; $7.95.

SEX, FAMILY, TRIBE — Get intimate with Ursula Le Guin, Ken Kesey, William Stafford, Colleen McElroy, Matt Groening, William Kittredge, Charles Johnson, and many more. #3. ISBN 0-936085-53-5; $7.95.

GOTTA EARN A LIVING — Know the work of two baker's dozen, including Norman Maclean, Kate Braid, Gary Snyder, David James Duncan, Teri Zipf, Sherman Alexie, Sibyl James, and Robin Cody. #4. ISBN 0-936085-54-1; $7.95.

BORDER & BOUNDARIES — Flee with the Bedouins, secede from the Union, travel with Michael Dorris, Diana Abu-Jaber, William Stafford, Sandra Scofield, Larry Colton. #5. ISBN 0-936085-58-4; $9.95.

KIDS' STUff — Definitely not for kids. Enjoy Mikal Gilmore, Sallie Tisdale, Sherman Alexie, Ann Rule, Virginia Euwer Wolff, Shani Mootoo, and others. #6. ISBN 0-936085-26-6; $9.95.

HEAD/WATERS — Immerse yourself in the flow of words, the watersheds of ideas. With David Duncan, Brenda Peterson, Gary Snyder, Lorian Hemingway, Susan Zwinger, and a wellspring of others. ISBN 0-936085-28-2; $9.95.

ASK FOR LEFT BANK BOOKS AT YOUR FAVORITE BOOKSTORE OR PHOTOCOPY THE ORDER FORM ON THE LAST PAGE.

LEFT BANK BOOKS
GREAT WRITING
GREAT READING
GREAT GIFTS
ORDER HERE

For yourself or any thoughtful friend.

Just photocopy this page, fill in the form, and send it today. Subscriptions to the next two Left Bank Books are $18*, postage paid, and begin with the next title published. Other titles are available individually; add $2.75 shipping for the first book and 75¢ for each additional book.

Send Left Bank to me at:

Send a gift subscription to:

I'd like the following editions (see previous page):

My order total is:

I've enclosed a check ☐ or Money Order ☐ — or charge my VISA ☐ or MC ☐; its number and expiration are:

VISA/MC orders may be placed at 503.621.3911 or mailed to Blue Heron Publishing, 24450 NW Hansen Road, Hillsboro, OR 97124.

*SUBSCRIPTION PRICES SUBJECT TO CHANGE WITHOUT NOTICE.